EVER

240 Poetry Prompts
from Two Sylvias Press

Kelli Russell Agodon & Annette Spaulding-Convy

Two Sylvias Press

Two Sylvias Press
PO Box 1524
Kingston, WA 98346
twosylviaspress@gmail.com

Cover Design: Kelli Russell Agodon
Book Design: Annette Spaulding-Convy

Created with the belief that great writing is good for the world,
Two Sylvias Press mixes modern technology, classic style, and
literary intellect with an eco-friendly heart. We draw our
inspiration from the poetic literary talent of Sylvia Plath and the
editorial business sense of Sylvia Beach. We are an independent
press dedicated to publishing the exceptional voices of writers.

For more information about Two Sylvias Press please visit:
www.twosylviaspress.com

First Edition. Created in the United States of America.

ISBN: 978-1-948767-10-1

Two Sylvias Press
www.twosylviaspress.com

Introduction

And by the way, everything in life is writable about if you have the outgoing guts to do it, and the imagination to improvise. — Sylvia Plath

Welcome to *Everything is Writable* from Two Sylvias Press!

This collection of poetry prompts arises from two of our popular online offerings created to inspire poets: *The Two Sylvias Press Advent Calendar of Poetry Prompts* and *The Two Sylvias Press April Prompts for National Poetry Month*. We have received many requests asking us to compile our prompts into a book, and so we have answered that request by creating *Everything is Writable* to assist you in your writing practice. Whether you are just beginning to write poetry or you are an established poet, these writing starts will offer fresh ideas and new directions for your work.

This book can be used on an individual level, in group writing sessions, in workshops, and in classrooms. The prompts are numbered from 1-240 and cover a wide array of topics and poetic styles. You can work through the prompts in numerical order or you can skip around if you like. For a more intuitive approach, try opening the book randomly and see what prompt you land on. There are endless creative ways to use these starts.

Here is our Two Sylvias advice for making the most of writing prompts:

- Be creative with the prompt. You don't need to follow it exactly, so allow your ideas and your poem to move in the direction of your inspiration.

A prompt about cotton candy might lead you to a fantastic poem on quantum theory. Be inventive.

- A single prompt can lead to many poems. Use each prompt more than one time because your mindset, mood, atmosphere, etc. will always lead to a different interpretation of the prompt. Don't hesitate to work your way through this book several times.

- If a particular prompt isn't working for you, move to a new prompt or get up from where you are writing and take a break, take a walk, or do another activity. Give the prompt another go later.

- Before you begin a prompt, read some poetry that inspires and excites you. Pick up a collection of one of your favorite poets, and read a few poems thoughtfully and carefully before you start writing—this can help get your own creativity flowing.

- Allow the first draft of your poem to be messy, disjointed, and "unpoetic." Sometimes the poetry that first comes out on a page can be less than ideal. Whatever material the prompt initially inspires can be revised and changed until you are happy with the resulting poem. Perhaps your final draft will not resemble the prompt at all, and that is absolutely fine.

- Most importantly, have fun as you write and turn off your internal editor. Sometimes wonderful poems arise when you write in a stream-of-consciousness style without a lot of editing as words and phrases pour out. You can always revise later.

It is our sincerest wish that *Everything is Writable* will inspire you to write more poems and that it will stretch you as a literary artist. You might find yourself writing poems on topics you've never written about before, and you might try some new poetic forms. Perhaps you may find that your poems are more daring, less self-conscious, and more experimental as you continue to develop your unique voice.

We have received some powerful feedback that our prompts have inspired not only chapbooks, but entire poetry collections. Since most full-length books contain 50-60 pages of poetry, if just 20% of these prompts lead to successful poems, you will have a manuscript ready for submission!

Remember what Sylvia Plath said: *Everything in life is writable.*

Be inspired and write often!

Kelli & Annette
Editors/Co-Founders of Two Sylvias Press

Writing is a job, a talent, but it's also the place to go in your head. It is the imaginary friend you drink your tea with in the afternoon.

— Ann Patchett

Prompt 1

NO LAUGHING MATTER

The Chinese philosopher Lau Tzu said, "As soon as you have a thought, laugh at it." Write a humorous poem about a serious subject: nuclear war, no money in your retirement account, job loss, illness, divorce, your house burning down, a spouse's affair, your inability to get along with your teenager. Begin your poem on a serious note and then surprise your reader with subtle and/or outright humor.

Prompt 2

MY FAVORITE MISTAKE

Before Edison discovered a light bulb that worked, he created almost 2,000 prototypes that ended up being mistakes. Write a poem about a failure in your life or mistake that you have made. Allow this poem to take a lighthearted and comical look at your mistake. Include the lesson that this failure taught you— the "I will never do that again" moment. Write about a failed relationship or the time you baked a cake with salt instead of sugar. Have some fun at your own expense!

Prompt 3

BREAKING THE FOURTH WALL

In theatre, when actors ignore the imaginary "wall" between themselves and the audience, it's called "breaking the fourth wall." For this prompt, write a poem where you (the poet or the speaker) address the reader directly. Make this a self-conscious poem in first person where you ask the reader questions and talk to him/her like an actor looking directly into the camera. If you're looking for a way to start the poem, begin with the line, "Reader, I see you..." and go from there.

Prompt 4

THE BEST OF THE WORST

An "ode" is a poem that is written in celebration and honor of someone or something. To give today's prompt a twist, write an ode that honors someone or something for being the absolute *worst!* You can put "worst" in your title, like "Ode to the Worst President" or you can leave "worst" out of your title and simply celebrate all of the yucky qualities of your subject: "Ode to Brussels Sprouts." Your poem will most likely be humorous as it lists why your subject is the best at being the worst!

Prompt 5

IT'S RAINING JAZZ

Put on music you never listen to (jazz, classical, rap, country, pop, etc.), and write a poem about the weather (or a big weather event your area has had in the last year—snow, wildfires, winds, rainstorms, etc.) and be inspired by the music you hear. See how/if the music changes the way you approach a poem and if the melody of the poem changes your mood. If you need an opening, begin the poem with, "Today, the weather sounds like…"

Prompt 6

THIS IS THE LONGING FOR THE AGE OF ASPARAGUS

Think of a song lyric and write it down on a piece of paper, then rewrite the same lyric 4 more times but changing words slightly. For example, if your lyric is "daydreaming and I'm thinking of you," you may write "day-drinking and I'm thinking of you," and "Daydreaming and I'm thinking of shoes," and "Daydreaming and I'm mixing the fruit." Write a poem that includes your newly changed lyrics.

Prompt 7

WONDERING ABOUT SUPERSTITIONS

Write a poem about a superstition or make up a superstition of your own. Maybe bad luck doesn't come in threes, but in nineties. Maybe it's not breaking a mirror that's seven years of bad luck, but binge-watching the TV show "Breaking Bad." For extra credit, use a line from Stevie Wonder's song "Superstition" in your poem and/or listen to it while you're writing.

Prompt 8

ICE CREAM IS BLISS

Write a poem where you take a cliché and give it a new twist ("kill two birds with one stone" becomes "feed two birds with one scone" or "curiosity killed the cat" become "ingenuity saved the cat"). Consider beginning your poem with the line "Some days I wonder if…"

Prompt 9

GOOD MORNING STARSHINE

An aubade is a poem (or a song) whose main theme deals with dawn, the beginning of the day. Traditionally, an aubade was concerned with lovers parting at daybreak. Write an aubade that celebrates something very ordinary in your usual morning routine: coffee, tea, tooth brushing, shower, letting the dog outside, perusing the news, doing a yoga stretch, etc. Use aubade in your title, for instance: "Aubade with Lotus Position" or "Aubade with Granola & Banana."

Prompt 10

PUNCTUATION? NO PROBLEM!!

Write a poem where you use punctuation in an unusual way. Maybe all of your lines end in an emdash—or maybe you (in a repetitive way) put everything in parentheses. What if you composed all of your lines as questions? Maybe the tilde (~) can find its way into your poem. There is no wrong (!!) way to do this;;;prompt as you explore *how* you can-use-punctuation in unique ways. . .

Prompt 11

WRECK A HAIKU

We all know the traditional Haiku form: three lines, usually with a nature theme, with the first line consisting of 5 syllables, the second line 7 syllables, and the third line 5 syllables. For today's prompt, consider "wrecking" and messing up this well-known form. Create an alternate Haiku—choose a theme (rather than nature, maybe the theme is science fiction) and a new form (rather than three lines, maybe five lines with syllable counts of 10/3/10/5/1). Once you have your made-up form, write several poems.

Prompt 12

FUZZLE, SNOUTFAIR, AND GROAK

Write a poem where you choose a word that is no longer heard much in general conversation. Use this word numerous times throughout your poem and, for a challenge, try to use it in every other line. Here are some ideas for odd words: *menacing, glacier, brouhaha, trophy, cupid, finagle, amble, buoy, charlatan, lollygag, fetching, kerfuffle, lambast, malarkey, moxie.* Use one of these or come up with your own uncommon word to repeat.

Prompt 13

THE GREATEST TEACHER, FAILURE IS

Write a poem where a character from *Star Wars* (R2D2, Luke Skywalker, Princess Leia, C3P0, Han Solo, Darth Vader, Yoda, etc.) makes an appearance. If you aren't a *Star Wars* fan, pick a character from any sci-fi book or movie. Perhaps your poem will explore why your Skywalker spouse has recently been acting like Emperor Palpatine.

Prompt 14

THERE ARE PLACES I REMEMBER

Think back to a place where you once lived and whose address you remember. Title your poem with this address (2201 Springbrook Lane) and write a poem that reminisces about a specific activity or event that occurred at this particular place. Your poem can be either joyful or serious. Describe the living space and the activity/event in vivid detail for your reader. Don't hesitate to be emotional.

Prompt 15

SASKATCHEWAN, SPARROW, SAW...

Write a poem that includes all of the following items: a vintage typewriter, the name of a well-known university or college, a kind of bird, a state or province, a piece of jewelry, a traffic sign, a carpenter's tool, and the name of a vintage record album. Begin your poem with the line "In a few days, I'll be..."

Prompt 16

GOGYOHKA: THE 5 LINE POEM

The Gogyohka is a Japanese poetic form made up of 5 lines, with each line consisting of a single phrase, and no restriction on the syllable count per line. For today's poem, write two Gogyohka. For the first poem, choose a nature theme—a day at the beach, an overnight in a forest, a hike, an inspiring sunrise, etc. For your second 5 line poem, write about food—a memorable meal, a trip to the grocery store, a restricted diet, a sensual dessert, or a humorous cooking mishap.

Prompt 17

WRITE YOUR TOWN DOWN

In her poem "Magnum Mysterium," Lucie Brock-Broido writes "I've lived in many places, it's odd / That I continue to waken in Nebraska." Write a poem that explores the details and specifics of your part of the world. Use street names, lesser-known tourist attractions, and names of flowers and birds in your area to center the poem in concrete nouns. You can also include other places where you would like to live and the details of that place.

Prompt 18

NATURAL SOLUTIONS

Write a poem that begins with an exploration of a personal issue or problem—maybe a divorce, a job loss, an unfulfilling relationship, the loss of someone, depression, anxiety, etc. Now, find hope, inspiration, and/or insight by also writing about something in nature that offers you some sort of "answer" to your issue—perhaps you find something on a beach, you see an erupting volcano, a shooting star, or a field of giant sunflowers.

Prompt 19

MR. DARCY OPENS A DAYCARE

Write a poem inspired by a character or characters from your favorite book or movie doing something you wouldn't expect. You could write a poem about a modern day Becky Thatcher (*Tom Sawyer*) hosting a Tupperware party, Holden Caulfield (*Catcher in the Rye*) using Tinder or a dating site, or choose someone from a more current novel such as Bernadette Fox (*Where'd You Go, Bernadette?*) being a Girl Scout leader. You are welcome to include yourself in the poem interacting with the character or you can write a persona poem that focuses only on your character.

Prompt 20

RED OR YELLOW OR PINK OR GREEN

Write a poem where all of the images in the poem are the same color. If you chose red, your poem may have a rooster, an apple, a pomegranate, a fire engine, a wheelbarrow, wine, a stop sign, etc. Slip the color subtly into your title. Consider writing your poem about one of these themes: loss, hope, love, nature, anger, or anxiety.

Prompt 21

HELLO, DALI

Begin a poem with this Salvador Dali quote, "Take me, I am the drug..." and use within your poem several titles of Dali's paintings: rose meditative, the endless enigma, bee around a pomegranate, the swallow's tail. Maybe look at several Dali paintings online before you begin writing, and then attempt to infuse your poem with the spirit of his work.

Prompt 22

BABY, YOU CAN DRIVE MY CAR

Compose a poem that incorporates as many of these words as you can: opera, pup, lady, that's, probe, dump, fish, bimbo, lettuce, naked, wizard, dunk, sandal, nanny, and scat. What do these words have in common? They are the names of car models that failed to be successful and were taken off the market. Make these words shine in a successful poem!

Prompt 23

LOW-TECH POEM
WITH HIGH-TECH WORDS

Write a poem that has nothing to do with technology or computers, but use some of the following high-tech, computer-related terms. For instance, write about last night's storm or sunset using words that one might expect to see in an article about Microsoft or Apple. Here's your list (and note that these words were "stolen" by high- tech): hibernate, access, host, log, zip, web, tag, storage, memory, refresh, script, remote, drive, batch, chip, shortcut, boot, burn, cookie, drag, frozen, input, link, menu, mouse.

Prompt 24

THE GOOD EARTH

Write a poem about the earth that uses at least three of these elements: a geometrical term such as "X ="; a line from a country song; a character from a novel; a type of cheese; a famous scientist, the name of a constellation; the name of a lesser-known body of water; and a line from a nursery rhyme. If you're having trouble beginning, consider, "When the world…"

Prompt 25

WALK (OR WRITE) LIKE AN EGYPTIAN

Use at least three symbols in a poem that are not letters or numbers. Incorporate some of the following: ©, ≠, @, <, π, ‖, ←, $, ∞. You can also copy and paste in rune symbols or hieroglyphs. Consider mentioning some elements of ancient archeology and/or ancient civilizations. For extra credit, use a Greek, Latin, Farsi, Hebrew, or Sanskrit word somewhere in your poem.

Prompt 26

BROKEN HEART,
BROKEBACK MOUNTAIN,
BREAKING UP IS HARD TO DO

Write a poem about a specific event in your past using various forms of the word "break," such as broken, broke, breaking. You can also use compound words, such as *heartbreak/break-up/breakdown* or titles of artwork or song titles, such as "Boulevard of Broken Dreams." For extra credit, include the words: *brake, braking, braked.*

Prompt 27

IS THERE ANYONE IN THE ECHO-VERSE....VERSE.....VERSE?

For this prompt, you will write a poem in which the first syllable of each line "echoes" the ending syllable of the previous line. Here is an example:

> It's   not   what   I   predic<u>ted</u>—
> <u>ted</u>dy   bears   on   the   <u>wall,</u>
> <u>wall</u>aby   magnets   on   your   fridge...

Write an "echo poem" that consists of at least twelve lines. If you would like some direction for a theme, consider writing your poem about a story that is currently in the news. Check a breaking news website right now, and choose a story that interests you....you....you.

Prompt 28

A POSTCARD TO MY GLABELLA

Write a poem in the form of a postcard (you can justify the margins to look like a postcard) and address it to a part of your body. You can be funny (flabby arms, hair that's too curly, etc.) or you can be serious (a body part afflicted by illness). Try to keep the poem short enough so that it could fit on an actual postcard. Allow yourself to be open and honest. (Note: glabella is the space between the eyebrows.)

Prompt 29

YOUR EYES ARE LIKE BLUEBERRY GRUNT

Use several of the following strange recipe names in a poem: Chocolate Therapy Brownies, Gunk on Noodles, Bubble and Squeak, Old Ladies on a Bun, Blueberry Grunt, Buddha's Delight, Spotted Dick. Consider writing a love poem (or a poem about romantic relationships) and give it a humorous bent by using these odd recipe names. Perhaps someone cooks "Old Ladies on a Bun" for a first date and then regrets it.

Prompt 30

CREATING SKY GARDENS
FOR YOUR CASTLE IN THE SKY

Write a poem where you build something in the sky or on another planet. Maybe you're planting dahlias in the clouds or serving martinis in the stratosphere. Maybe you want to build an ice cream shop on Saturn or an artist colony on the moon. Place manmade and natural items from Earth into a new environment and see where your poem goes.

Prompt 31

DESPERATELY SEEKING SOLITUDE

Write a poem that includes a personal ad to someone or something. Maybe it's "married woman poet seeks muse for long hours of writing together" or "single man seeks downtime." You can write a personal ad to the perfect margarita or for something more serious, such as "searching for the antidote to grief." You are welcome to make your poem as funny or as serious as you like—or maybe a bit of both.

Prompt 32

IT'S NEVER TOO LATE

Write a poem in the third person (he/she/they/it) where the speaker of your poem is trying to do something difficult. Maybe a woman is trying to learn how to moonwalk or a man is learning how to swim at age 60 with a deep fear of water. Maybe you want to write about a child trying to talk with the photo of her dead grandma. Observe the moment in your mind, and then show the scene in your poem.

Prompt 33

ONE TEASPOON
OF CUSTODY BATTLE

Write a "How To" poem in the form of a recipe, but do not mention food. Perhaps you've got the ingredients for "A Divorce" (1 cup of an affair, 2 tsp of not listening), or maybe you'll write the recipe for "How To Get Over a Death" or "How to Build a Peaceful World." The poem can be as surreal, funny, or strange as you would like. For help, find a recipe (online or from a cookbook) to use as a template.

Prompt 34

MY SAFFRON MITTENS

Write a poem consisting of five short stanzas. In the 1st and 5th stanzas use an odd color, like vermillion, beryl, chartreuse, etc. In the 2nd stanza mention a deceased celebrity. In the 3rd stanza mention a food that you personally dislike, and in the 4th stanza, add in an article of clothing or an accessory that you would wear in winter.

Prompt 35

SIMPLIFY IT

Write a poem that is eight to twelve lines long. Limit yourself to only four words per line or less. Vary the words per line—two words, then four words, then one word, then a line with no words, etc. To create an interesting contrast in this poem, choose a theme that is complex, but write about it sparingly—the political climate in America, global climate change, quantum physics, the origin of intelligent life, etc.

Prompt 36

START FROM THE END

Set your timer for 10-15 minutes and write a quick poem about something you have recently observed (a goose in a field, a woman in a yellow raincoat, etc.). Write quickly, mentioning specific details using as many active verbs as you can (burning, running, dancing, stealing, sailing). When you are finished, rewrite your poem making the last line your first line, the second to the last line, your second line, and so on. See if you like the poem with the reversed line order, and if you don't like it, feel free to leave your poem in its original form.

Prompt 37

TWO POLITICIANS WALK INTO A BAR

Write a poem in which a political figure from the past interacts with a current living politician. Maybe the past figure berates and lectures the current figure or maybe congratulates him or her. Maybe they have a drink together or have a fist-fight or maybe they solve a current crisis. What might George Washington say to Donald Trump? Would Gandhi advise Boris Johnson? Would Cleopatra high-five Hillary Clinton?

Prompt 38

IN THE AGE OF AQUARIUS
I LEARNED TO RIDE A BIKE

Aimee Nezhukumatathil writes *The summer I learned to make successful jam, I felt full of secrets...* in her poem "Last Summer of Singledom." Think about something you once learned to do (play the guitar, boil an egg, drive a car, etc.), and write a poem where you explore that experience using imagery of the time period to show your age and the decade. For extra credit, mention a secret in the poem.

Prompt 39

WHAT DREAMS MAY COME

Write a poem that begins in a dream and ends up in real life. Be sure to include surreal and odd images that might be found in a dream, such as a person flying, arriving at a job (or school) naked, running in slow motion, or bizarre events—a talking hen or someone juggling jello or an alien invasion.

Prompt 40

OH SWEET RESTRICTION

This prompt celebrates structure and guidelines. Write a poem that is ten lines long. Do not exceed ten words per line. Your theme is a frightening experience you once had. In lines 2, 5, and 9 mention a color. In line 3 reference a piece of furniture (chair, table, bed, etc.), and in line 1 include a day of the week or a month or a specific year (1986, etc). In line 10 include a non-English word (adios, faux pas, alma mater, status quo, etc.). In your poem's title, include a proper noun (the name of a person, place, planet, etc.). Try to follow the rules exactly!

Prompt 41

A POCKETFUL OF NIRVANA

Write a poem that makes use of religious and spiritual terms, but whose topic has nothing to do with religion or spirituality. Use these terms in interesting and fresh ways: "his eyes are fountains of holy water" or "she keeps track of her mistakes on rosary beads." Choose several of the following religious and spiritual words (or come up with some on your own) to use creatively in your poem: karma, rosary, temple, angel, afterlife, chakra, holy water, mantra, nirvana, shaman, totem animal, saint, aura, hymn, baptism.

Prompt 42

POE PLACES PLACEMATS AROUND THE PENTAGON

In an old London churchyard, there is an ash tree surrounded by hundreds of gravestones placed there by author Thomas Hardy. The tree is named "The Hardy Tree." Write a poem where a famous poet, author, or celebrity creates a landmark made of unique things. Maybe Walt Whitman pins dead butterflies to lilac bushes or Mark Twain ties pocket watches onto fences.

Prompt 43

RED RED WINE

Persian writer Omar Khayyam famously said that happiness/contentment for him was simply "a book of verses underneath a bough, a jug of wine, a loaf of bread, and thou." As a play on Khayyam's quote, write a poem that mentions a specific book of poems, a type of wine, a kind of bread, and a specific person. For instance, *Leaves of Grass*, Pinot Noir, sourdough, and Mr. Rogers.

Prompt 44

IN HIGH GEAR

Use some of the following automotive terms in a poem about a romantic relationship: beltline, torque, knock, limited slip, turbocharged, blip the throttle, pushrod, oversteer, opposite lock, double clutching, suspension, exhaust, strut, filter, harmonic balancer, converter. If you need help beginning your poem: "Usually I'm in the driver's seat, but…"

Prompt 45

EASY-BAKE OVEN
OR MY LITTLE PONY?

Think about one of your favorite toys from childhood and recall a specific memory that involves this toy. Write a poem about this toy and memory or write a poem that simply mentions the toy and memory. To give yourself some creative restriction, end each line with a word that ends in "ing"—walking, something, bring, laughing, etc. For extra credit mention an animal, a month, and an article of clothing.

Prompt 46

WITH FLYING COLORS

Write a poem where every line has a color in it. The color does not have to be spelled the way you would expect: "red" or "read," "blue" or "blew," etc. The color can also be within a word "Brownsville" or "greenhouse" or "goldmine." The poem can be about any topic, but reference a painter or painting. If you're having trouble beginning, consider: "In the winter, I hold…"

Prompt 47

THANK YOU SO MUCH
FOR THE FISH STICKS

Write a poem where a lover brings you something unexpected: an old shoe, a box of broken eggshells, a feather boa, a broken typewriter, a wooden Buddha, a stolen painting, a box of Apple Jacks cereal, a wilted oregano plant, etc. In your poem, describe what you do with the object and how you feel about it. For extra credit, compose your poem in tercets (three line stanzas).

Prompt 48

I FOOLED AROUND
AND FELL IN LOVE

Write a poem where the speaker of your poem or a character in your poem does something really foolish that ends up with a positive outcome. Maybe a woman in your poem decides to quit her job because she hates the wall art in her office and ends up becoming a famous painter, or maybe you write about someone selling his great aunt's cameo collection to a woman he ends up falling in love with. You can also choose something foolish you've done in your life that didn't work out well, and give it a new positive twist.

Prompt 49

HEAVY METAL

Write a poem in which you use the following terms from the craft of blacksmithing (creating objects from iron): temper, cast, brake, flux, scale, quench, drawing, blast, harden, bloom, cope, slush, file, dip, recovery, core, blowing. Use these metalworking words in a poem that deals with a difficult circumstance you have gone through. Play with all of the various double meanings of these terms—a blacksmith's "file" tool for smoothing a metal surface can become the secret "file" you find on your spouse's computer.

Prompt 50

REJECTION IS A CHALLENGE!

Write a poem about a rejection. This could be a poetry rejection, a romantic rejection, application for a job rejection, friendship rejection, etc. Compose your rejection poem in one continuous sentence, using lots of conjunctions and commas or semicolons—whatever you need to keep your flow. Use some of the following words: plastic, footprints, cushion, cocktail, rumor, minor, lucky, lemon, magic, spin, paper.

Prompt 51

SYLVIA KNOWS SADNESS

Write a poem where you answer the question asked by Sylvia Plath in her poem, "Three Women," *What pains, what sorrows must I be mothering?* Consider what sadness (or sad thought) you find yourself always having to care for. Feel free to use images from motherhood, parenthood, or mother nature. Maybe use "Today I mother..." as your opening line. For extra credit, reference Sylvia Plath in your poem.

Prompt 52

I'VE GOT YOUR NUMBER

Write a ten line poem where each line begins with a number and/or a word that sounds like a number: one/won, two/to/too, three, four/for, eight/ate, twenty-one, million, etc.) The numbers do not have to be in order and can be repeated with variations. Consider writing about a recent event that left you feeling confused or out of sorts.

Prompt 53

IF THIS, THEN THAT

Write a fantasy poem about any topic of your choosing using the "if, then" structure. For example, "If the moon tastes like melons, then the stars must be strawberries" or "If I can swallow the sea, then the world must know how thirsty I am." Allow your writing to move in many different directions and see how fantastical you can make your poem.

Prompt 54

I SAW STRANGE LIGHTS AT AREA 51

Write a poem that includes a conspiracy theory in it. The conspiracy theory can be the main subject of the poem or it can be casually mentioned. Here are a few conspiracies to consider (or look on the internet for some other ideas): Elvis is still alive, the moon landing was faked, extraterrestrials live among us, Paul McCartney died in 1966 and was replaced by a look-alike

Prompt 55

TAKE YOUR DOGMA FOR A WALK

Think about an encounter you have had with religion or spirituality. Maybe you went on a great Zen retreat or maybe you have too much Catholic guilt from childhood. Write a poem about an experience with religion/spirituality (it can be positive or negative) that has left an impact on you. Don't be afraid to rant and scream. Don't be afraid to offer praise and thanks.

Prompt 56

RUNNING IN CIRCLES

Draw 10 circles on a piece of paper. Now quickly turn each circle into an image (sun, peace sign, etc.). Once you have 10 images, choose at least five of these to include in your poem. Write a poem that is at least fifteen lines long. Challenge yourself by writing in couplets.

Prompt 57

CLICHÉ GOT YOUR TONGUE?

Write a poem that breaks the rules! Use clichés in a creative way—perhaps as dialogue or in unexpected, odd places in your poem. Surprise your reader by using these tired phrases in a fresh manner. Here are some clichés to consider adding to your poem (use at least four): read between the lines, only time will tell, nerves of steel, ugly as sin, opposites attract, calm before the storm, diamond in the rough, time flies, old as the hills, kiss and make-up, what goes around comes around, every cloud has a silver lining.

Prompt 58

THOMAS EDISON DOES REGGAE

Write a poem about a famous singer or scientist. If you chose to write about a singer, put him/her in a scientific environment (maybe a chemistry lab or at NASA). If you chose to write about a scientist, put him/her in a musical environment (maybe on stage doing karaoke or on the beach with a guitar). Allow science and song to inform your poem.

Prompt 59

MAKE A WISH, BABY…
AND I WILL MAKE IT COME TRUE

Write a poem that consists of a wish or many
wishes in a row. Perhaps a big wish for world
peace, a reverse in climate change, or
something lighter, like fewer dishes in the sink at
night or for someone to surprise you with cake.
Let the poem meander through different
images, or for an extra challenge, include a wish
in every other line. Allow stream-of-
consciousness to run through this poem, not
worrying about where the poem is going or
whether it makes sense.

Prompt 60

IT'S SHOWTIME!

Choose a movie that you have recently seen (or an older favorite movie) and quickly write down twenty words you associate with the storyline of this particular film. If you choose *The Wizard of Oz*, your list might be: yellow, road, witch, lion, emerald, tornado, poppies, balloon, farm, aunt, etc. Next, read over your list and circle twelve to fifteen words that appeal to you most and compose your poem using them, but write about something that is not at all connected to the movie.

Prompt 61

LOCATION, LOCATION, LOCATION

Open up Google maps to the entire US or country of your choice (or find a print map in an atlas). Close your eyes and randomly touch the screen (or page). Scroll in and look at some of the place names (Smallville, Rhubarb Lake, Happy Valley, Maple Mt., etc.) Use these place names in your poem. Maybe do some quick research about the area. You don't have to be true to the facts—be creative with these place names.

Prompt 62

IT'S A MARVELOUS NIGHT
FOR A MOONDANCE

Write a poem that includes all of these types of moons: Blood Moon (red glow), Supermoon (appears larger than usual), Blue Moon (a month with two full moons), Harvest Moon (full moon that occurs in September), and Wolf Moon (the first full moon in January). Consider writing a 5 stanza poem and beginning each stanza with the phrase: "On the night of (name of moon)..." For instance, stanza 1 could begin, "On the night of the Wolf Moon...." and stanza 2, "On the night of the Supermoon..." etc, using each of the moons mentioned above for your 5 stanzas.

Prompt 63

SHE SEES SEASHELLS
NOT ON THE SEASHORE

Roudoudous are French candies that are created when a fruity syrup is drizzled and left to harden in an actual seashell. Write a poem where seashells are used for something surprising. You can focus on one thing—for instance, a seashell dress and its owner, or maybe your poem is a scene where you are walking through an urban environment to discover seashells as doorknobs or hubcaps.

Prompt 64

MY DEAREST PERSIMMON

Write a poem that is a fan letter to your favorite food. Maybe it's "Postcard to Potato Chips," "Dear Homemade Guacamole," "Memo to Meatloaf," "Love Letter to Chicken Dinner." Have the poem be an over-the-top expression of love to the deliciousness of any food item of your choice. Bring in specific experiences (a special birthday cake, childhood memories, first experiences, seeing it on the menu during a dinner out, etc.) along with comparisons to positive events or images. For extra credit, (and extra fun) eat the food while you're writing the poem.

Prompt 65

BEETS, BEEF, AND BEER

Write a poem that uses groups of three words which are similar in spelling: plan / plant / planet, love / glove / clove, short / shot / shirt, owl /owe / ode, see / sea / seed, three / tree / free, water / waiter / watcher, flower / flow / lower, etc. Use at least two of the above groups in your poem or come up with your own groupings of similarly spelled words. Place the setting of your poem in a specific season, and consider mentioning the season in your title.

Prompt 66

WHILE MY GUITAR GENTLY WEEPS

Write a poem in which a musical instrument is ruined—by fire, by earthquake, by being dropped out of a window, or something else you imagine. Write about the beauty of the destruction and the sounds the instrument makes as it is being destroyed. Maybe use a simile or metaphor to compare the sound of the instrument being destroyed to something surprising: a mosquito in a bug zapper or coins in the dryer.

Prompt 67

POSTCARDS FROM THE EDGE

Write a poem that begins with the phrase "When I saw the postmark from (insert place here), I knew…" Perhaps your postmark is from London, Nashville, Beijing, Littleville, Toronto, etc. The contents of your poem might be completely made up ("When I saw the postmark from Mars, I knew that you were out of my life forever…") or maybe you once received a letter that had a dramatic effect on you. Include the following words in your poem: hand, minute, air, silver, billboard.

Prompt 68

CHOOSE YOUR WEAPON

Write a four-stanza poem and begin each stanza with the phrase "Each day I choose…" Try not to overthink this poem, but rather, allow the images and phrases to flow unedited. After you have written the poem, reread it to see how the poem reads if you remove the "Each day I choose…" phrase. As you revise, leave "Each day I choose…" in your poem or remove it or modify it.

Prompt 69

WHAT'S A HOMOGRAPH?

Write a poem using homographs (words spelled the same but pronounced differently depending on meaning): buffet (tossed or meal), bass (tone or fish), bow (bend or branch), does (do or deer), moped (sad or motorcycle), entrance (entry or bewitch), lead (go first or metal), minute (time or small), tear (rip or cry), wind (turn or weather). Use at least four sets of these homographs in your poem. You can search the internet for other examples.

Prompt 70

GRASS IN *LEAVES OF GRASS*

Librarians over the years have reported finding some bizarre things left in library books: $100 bills, credit cards, pressed marijuana leaves, home pregnancy tests, bacon, pickles, Kraft Singles, divorce papers, drivers licenses, naked photos, and love letters. Compose a poem in which a surprising object is found inside a specific book—this object can be humorous, poignant, or shocking. Include the title of the book in your poem's title.

Prompt 71

HE SAID / SHE SAID

Write a poem consisting of 4 stanzas with 4 lines in each stanza. Imagine a disagreement between a man and a woman (lovers, spouses, friends, father and daughter, mother and son, etc.) and create a sort of "stanza dialogue" with stanza 1 and 3 beginning with "He said..." and stanzas 2 and 4 beginning with "She said..." For instance stanza 1 could start: "He said *the falling snow is depressing, so frozen...*" and stanza 2 could begin "She said *but I love how white draws me inward...*" etc.

Prompt 72

BLURRY MEMORIES
WITH CONCRETE MOMENTS

Write a poem about something you have a hazy memory of—you can't quite remember all of the details. Maybe this event is the death of someone close to you or a simple daily event, such as "what did I have for dinner on November 3rd?" Fill in the missing parts you don't remember with concrete images. For example, "I wore a denim jacket with a brown patch on the sleeve." You can begin the poem with "I remember" and then remove "I remember" when you revise.

Prompt 73

WHAT THE ARMADILLO WHISPERED

Close your eyes and think of an animal. This animal has come to you to share a secret—what does it say? Imagine the animal talking to you and write down its words. If you don't know how to begin, try starting with the name of the animal, such as "When the wolf speaks…"

Prompt 74

A-LIST

Write a list poem where every line begins with the word, "America…" then finish each line with an image or action. For example, you could write, "America wears sweatpants when it can't find its pantsuit" and "America asks me to drive the roads others have forgotten." (Also, feel free to substitute another country or city such as *Seattle, Italy, Miami*, etc. instead of *America*, if you wish.)

Prompt 75

CHILL OUT

Take some time to reflect on the activities you do in order to lessen your tension and anxiety. Do you take a walk, sit down and breathe deeply, enjoy a hot bath, read an inspiring book, meditate, sit in your favorite chair and drink a cup of herbal tea or red wine? Come up with two ways that you chill out when you are tense or anxious and write a poem that explores the ways that you find peace in an overly stressed-out world. Create an experience for your readers of total serenity as they take in your poem.

Prompt 76

DEAR MARVIN,
YOU'RE A TINY PLANET

Write a poem in which you name an asteroid for someone you know. Maybe you are naming the asteroid for someone who is genuinely "stellar" and wonderful or perhaps you are naming the asteroid for someone who is too "spacey" in your relationship. Use several or all of the following words: chart, fraction, saint, skin, bonfire, wheel, breakfast, dim, footnote.

Prompt 77

SOUP'S ON!

Write a poem in which soup plays a major role. Think about your associations with "homemade soup," "Ramen," "Cup O Noodles," "Pho," or "Campbell's Soup." Consider the following "soupy" expressions: "alphabet soup," "soup kitchen," "primordial soup," "stone soup, "fog as thick as pea soup." Maybe your poem will be about nurturing and childhood or how the goopiness of condensed cream of mushroom soup is like a current relationship.

Prompt 78

THE ART OF LISTENING

Stop what you are doing and listen to the sounds around you—maybe if you are home alone, you can hear the fridge buzzing or the tick of a clock. If you are at work, maybe you overhear your coworkers chatting. If you are in a coffee shop, perhaps you hear the espresso machine and background music. Write a poem focusing on the sounds you hear right now, and include the idea of being frightened.

Prompt 79

JUST DESSERTS

Write a poem that uses several of these interesting names of desserts, but don't write about desserts or food. Use the names creatively to refer to things that are not in the culinary world. Feel free to modify these names. Here's your list: summer berry grunt, tiny raspberry fools, rhubarb mess, orange buckle, treacle sponge, hobnobs, fat rascals, dead man's leg, black bun, pond pudding. For extra credit, write your poem about an issue you are having at work or something that needs fixing around your house.

Prompt 80

THAT'S SO RANDOM!

Some very good poems are filled with random elements that take the reader on an entertaining and crazy journey. Write a poem that uses *all* of the following random elements (write unedited so that your subconscious will create the connections): computer, shoes, vanilla, marriage, universe, stoplight, catbox, dictionary, bench, maple syrup, eye, snail, medicine, statue, poison ivy, pocket, ocean, queen, cigarette.

Prompt 81

12 WORDS IN WHATEVER ORDER

Write a 12 line poem that includes one of these words in each of the 12 lines: *moonshine, together, bread, survive, hook, snap, romance, fracture, barefoot, watercolor, iron, fever.* The words can be in any order, just make sure there is one of these words in each line. For extra credit, place the words at the end or beginning of each of the lines.

Prompt 82

I'M A MYSTERY WRAPPED
IN AN ENIGMA

Write a poem where each line tells something about you most people don't know. Do you have a Facebook account with a fake name? Do you hide something you shouldn't have in your car or in a secret place in your house? Even though you're married, do you buy coffee from a certain barista because you get a pang of excitement when s/he smiles at you? If you're having trouble beginning, consider, "You would be shocked if you knew…"

Prompt 83

RANTING & RAVING OVER NOTHING

Write a rant poem about something silly or something no one really cares about: did Kevin Bacon do his own dancing in the *Footloose* movie, should pizza be called "God's food," how many people dislike the color pink, why do dogs eat grass, did Dolly Parton get a facelift, etc. Try writing the first draft of your rant poem without any punctuation.

Prompt 84

SQUEAKY FEETS, SLIPPERY FINGERS, AND THEY ALL WORE MASKS

In Newport, Oregon, raccoons broke into an art gallery through a vent then became trapped inside. Police helped free the animals, but jokingly wrote in their report: *It was a gang of thieves with colorful nicknames, including "Squeaky Feets."* Write a poem where animals are somewhere they shouldn't be, doing something they shouldn't be doing. For extra credit, give them creative nicknames.

Prompt 85

SUNDOWN, YOU BETTER TAKE CARE

Imagine that it's December—the darkest time of the year. Write a poem that incorporates some of the following terms for darkness. For extra credit, challenge yourself to use these words in a creative way in a poem that is actually about a joyous occasion. Here's your list: dusk, shade, shadow, blackout, dim, smoky, unlit, twilight, cloudiness, obscure, cover.

Prompt 86

TRAINS, PLANES AND AUTOMOBILES

Studies by the Harvard sociologist Mario Luis Small have determined that we may confide in strangers more than we realize, especially when we are traveling. For this prompt, choose a type of transportation—plane, bus, train, ferry boat, cab, etc. and write a poem where you tell a stranger a secret. The poem can be in first or third person focusing on a real secret you have or something completely made up. Use sounds and images from the type of transportation you choose to keep your reader grounded in the scene.

Prompt 87

LOVE, LOVE ME DO

The Ancient Greeks had six different words for the concept of "love." As you look over this list of "loves," choose the one that you relate to the least and compose a poem that explores this type of love. Try writing this poem in a prose poem format—a block of text that doesn't concern itself with line breaks, but looks like a small paragraph on the page. You can always revise your prose poem later and break it into specific lines and stanzas. Here are the types of love: sexual passion, deep friendship, playful affection that is childlike, universal love for everyone, longstanding and patient love, and love of self.

Prompt 88

QUESTION EVERYTHING?

Begin your poem by coming up with a title that is a question (e.g. Why Is Everyone So Busy?). Make each line of your poem a question that continues to explore your title (for example, "Why are we all so tired?"). Aim for 8-12 lines of questions. For the last line, don't ask a question, but make a statement. Perhaps answer your title question or create a last line that is only somewhat related to the rest of the poem ("I am a frog, alone in a pond.").

Prompt 89

HOPE SPRINGS

The poet Lucille Clifton once said, "Writing is a way of continuing to hope." Think of a situation in your life or in the world that can feel "hopeless" to you. Write a poem that explores this sense of hopelessness, but as the poem progresses, arrive at a feeling of "hope." Maybe you are distressed by the dysfunction in politics or rampant violence in society—find what gives you hope in these situations and conclude your poem on a positive note.

Prompt 90

HE'S SO HAREBRAINED!

Choose a favorite odd word, something fun like "banana," "bonanza," "filibuster," "slapdash," etc. Now use that word as many times in a poem as you can. Have the poem be about something not connected to the meaning of the word. For example, if you choose "filibuster" maybe your poem is about a constellation and has nothing to do with politics. Use your chosen word in new and surprising ways.

Prompt 91

MY TATTOO IS TABOO

Write a poem that uses five or more of these words: *tattoo, tinfoil, shoelace, cockleshell, hazard, queen, dazzle, bellow, sprout, fever, humor, shallow, quibble*. If you are looking for a topic to write about, maybe explore a subject that makes you feel vulnerable. Perhaps you worry about the fate of the planet or flying in a jet makes you nervous. Or write about something you feel you shouldn't be writing about.

Prompt 92

THE WONDER YEARS

Write a poem where you wonder about several different things in your poem. Maybe you wonder about life on another planet, if you have enough money for retirement, if fossil fuels will be a thing of the past, or what time the mail carrier will come today. Allow the poem to flow into several different thoughts—move from the large personal "will I make it through this year?" to the specific personal "are we out of sugar?" to the large global "how is the rest of the world doing?" to the specific global "will the ground-cuckoo of southern Sumatra become extinct?"

Prompt 93

NEVER WRITE ABOUT GRANDMAS OR KITTIES OR PETUNIAS!

In the poetry world there are sometimes strange rules about topics that you aren't supposed to write about because of sentimentality and "sweetness." So, to break this rule, write a poem about your grandma, your pet, or your favorite flower, BUT, make this poem edgy, dark, obnoxious, shocking—anything but cute and sweet. Maybe grandma is currently in prison for embezzling funds from the company where she was a bookkeeper for thirty years.

Prompt 94

JUST DON'T

Write a poem in which you tell someone not to do something: "Please don't call me honey/sir/ma'am" or "Please don't order oysters." Allow the poem to be a rant and/or humorous as it lists its "don'ts." Maybe write the poem for a specific person or address the poem to a general "you." For extra credit, write the poem in a loose 14-line sonnet form.

Prompt 95

HOW THE BLEW / THE OCEAN BLUE

Write a poem where you end every line with words that are homophones—words that sound the same but are spelled differently (blue / blew, through / threw / drive-thru, etc.) or end all of your lines using the same last three letters such as "ion" (distraction / definition/action, etc.) Use one of the words or ending letters in the title of your poem.

Prompt 96

OPPOSITES ATTRACT

Write a ten line poem and in each line include two opposite words. You can be creative with how you use the words, for instance "love/hate" can turn into "My lover hates for me to be late." Use the following opposites and/or come up with some of your own: ice / fire; awake / asleep; bitter / sweet; lost / found; clear / cloudy; outer / inner; everything / nothing; start / stop; full / empty; far / near; deep / shallow; crazy / sane.

Prompt 97

WAITING FOR A GIRL LIKE YOU

Elizabeth Bishop's poem "In the Waiting Room," is about her memory of waiting for her aunt at the dentist's office when she was 6 years old. The poem meanders through what she sees there—a *National Geographic* magazine, adults, overcoats, lamps, as well as deep thoughts about life and the world. Write a poem where, as you wait for someone, you consider this strange life where we all roam on a rotating planet. Feel free to include your deep thoughts about life, death, time, and the universe along with the concrete details of what's around you as you wait.

Prompt 98

LET THERE BE GHOSTS

Write a poem in the voice of a dead poet, artist, or a relative. Either have him/her speak about an issue in the world or create a scene where he/she converses with you directly throughout the poem. Maybe Georgia O'Keeffe is concerned about the environment, Sylvia Plath has a deep hope for good healthcare, or your dead grandmother wants to talk about pandemics—give voice to the dead making sure to include images throughout your work.

Prompt 99

AFTER THREE MARTINIS, RAINBOWS ARE EVERWHERE

Write a poem that continuously repeats a famous or well-known image: red wheelbarrow, white dove, peace sign, stop sign, yin/yang, Mr. Yuk, smiley face, rainbow, under construction, one way, tree of life, Celtic cross, etc. For extra credit, have the speaker of the poem or the subject of the poem be in some sort of altered state: drunk, coming out of anesthetic, awakened in the middle of the night, accidently having ingested a cannabis candy, etc.

Prompt 100

IT'S IN THE STARS

Write a poem in which you imagine a visit to an astrologer, a psychic, or a fortune teller (tarot reader, palm reader, crystal ball gazer). Begin by quickly writing out 7 things that the "reader" tells you about your future. Don't edit, but let these "predictions" flow freely from your subconscious. It's ok if they are prose sentences. Now use these "predictions" as material for your poem. Use one, some, or all of them.

Prompt 101

HOLIDAY INN

Write a poem that includes at least 6 of these words: horoscope, smuggle, suspicion, invention, battle, connected, escape, bubbling, agate, mirage, open-heart surgery, boomerang, dazzling. Have the poem take place in a hotel/motel or on a road trip. If you need a little help starting out, consider the opening line, "When I opened the ..."

Prompt 102

HAUNTED BEACH BLANKET BINGO

Write a poem where an imaginary figure interacts with you. Have the poem take place in a location you would not expect to have an imaginary interaction (the mall, on a crowded bus, in the middle of summer under a sun umbrella, etc.) Maybe Little Red Riding Hood asks you for money for a political cause or an alien from a planet in the Pleiades is working the drive-thru window at Wendy's. Try to incorporate as many of these words as possible into your poem: breakfast, pop, party, cigarette, taste, karaoke, slim, buttonhole.

Prompt 103

I'VE GOT A SECRET

Write a poem where you tell the reader a secret. It could be *your* secret or the secret of someone else. Maybe it's a secret you just made up. If you're struggling to think of secrets, maybe these actual secrets will inspire you: Winston Churchill once ordered a cover-up of a UFO sighting, the FBI spent a month spying on John Lennon, Grand Central Station has a secret platform (Track 61) for well-to-do travelers (and presidents) that isn't on any map.

Prompt 104

DYSTOPIAN OR UTOPIAN?

Write a poem that takes place 100 years from now. What does the world look like? What new technologies are there? Are humans completely living an apocalyptic existence fighting zombies and aliens? Has humanity reached an ideal state where all wealth is shared with hunger and poverty no longer a reality? Feel free to be as inventive as you like—from cars that fly or drive themselves to living on other planets (or vacationing there). Or maybe we've destroyed most of the earth and we live in tents made from the ashes of forest fires. Wherever your imagination goes with this world, let it.

Prompt 105

DON'T BE AFRAID OF BEING SCARED

Madame Curie famously said, "Nothing in life is to be feared, it is only to be understood." Think about the things in life you fear most and/or the things that are real phobias for you. Maybe you absolutely fear death or spiders or heights or clowns or poverty or water, etc. Choose one of these very real fears and write a poem in which you attempt to "understand" this fear—maybe you will write a poem about a beautiful garden spider making a web in your kitchen window or maybe how losing your job might be a relief and could result in you simplifying your life.

Prompt 106

SHOUT, SHOUT LET IT ALL OUT

Write a poem in which an inanimate object is shouting something. Your poem can be humorous or serious, or perhaps have elements of both. Maybe your car is shouting that it is tired of the rattle every time it goes over 50 mph or maybe your wedding ring is shouting that some elements of your relationship need to be dealt with and reconsidered. What would the Statue of Liberty shout? What might the moon or Antarctica shout? Consider using italics for the various words and phrases your chosen object might shout.

Prompt 107

WRECK A POEM

Think of some famous poem titles and by changing one letter, create a new title (or "wreck" the title as it is known on social media). *The Raven* becomes *The Haven*; *The Road Not Taken* is *The Toad Not Taken*; *Dover Beach* becomes *Lover Beach*; *Red, Red Rose* is *Red, Red Nose*. So, wreck a famous poem title and then write a poem using your wrecked title. Have fun!

Prompt 108

BRAND YOUR POEM

Write a poem in which you mention many things by their brand names. Reference a few of the following: a chain store (Macy's, Home Depot, Starbucks, etc.), a food/drink (Oreos, Doritos, Kevita Kombucha, 7up, etc.), a car (Prius, Mustang, Kia, etc.), a medicine (Advil, Preparation H, Tums, etc.), an electronic device (iPhone, Android, Dell, etc.), a candy (M&Ms, Tic-Tacs, Gummi Bears, Butterfinger, etc.) and a makeup brand (Revlon, CoverGirl, L'Oreal, etc.). Your poem can be lighthearted or critical of society.

Prompt 109

AND THE RABBIT BLESSED US

Write a poem about a specific event (a breakup, a wedding, a New Year's Eve party, etc.) that uses images that you wouldn't expect to see in those events. Create images that will surprise your reader and/or are the opposite of what someone would expect. Maybe the minister at a wedding is wearing a rabbit costume. Maybe if your poem is about a breakup, the couple is kissing, and they realize the neighbor is locked in their bathroom.

Prompt 110

LETTERING IN POETRY

Choose a letter of the alphabet. Write a poem where every line begins and/or ends with that letter. The subject of the poem can be about anything you wish, but if you need help getting started, write the poem as a letter to someone about an issue you are struggling with or about an unbelievable thing that recently happened to you.

Prompt 111

EINSTEIN CALCULATES CALORIES BURNED IN ZUMBA CLASS

Write a persona poem in the voice of an historical figure who has time-traveled to this year and is shocked by what s/he sees. To begin, ask yourself: What would s/he say about the state of the world, the new technology, pop culture, politics, etc.? Begin your poem with the historical figure asking a question. Extra credit: include a household appliance, a sea creature, and the name of a chain store.

Prompt 112

IT'S HIP TO BE SQUARE

Write a poem where you have several stanzas that are as square-shaped as possible so your poem looks as if you have put small post-it notes over your page. Each of these square stanzas should include small messages you want to tell someone. Examples may be "Michelle, sometimes I still think/about your thigh-high black boots" or "On dark mornings, father, I still see you/in the fog." You can arrange these square stanzas vertically, or use the "text box" in MS Word to place them all around the page.

Prompt 113

CREATIVE ANACHRONISM OR INTENTIONAL TIMELINE GOOFS

Here are two famous timeline mistakes in movies: *Robin Hood: Prince of Thieves* features a telescope that was invented 600 years later and *Raiders of the Lost Ark* shows a map with 1981 country borders in its 1936 setting. Write a poem that sneaks in two intentional timeline errors. Maybe a kid in the 1980s watches a DVD or Queen Victoria drinks a bourbon & 7Up or great grandma buckles up her seatbelt in the Model T. Be subtle and creative.

Prompt 114

PAINT WITH WORDS

Think of a well-known painting that you love.
What draws you to it? Write a poem in which
you find yourself in this painting—perhaps you
are the Mona Lisa, maybe you are walking
through a Georgia O'Keeffe landscape with
flowers and skulls, or maybe you are trapped in
one of Mondrian's squares. As your poem
unfolds, perhaps the artist himself/herself makes
an appearance. Allow your imagination to have
fun and fill your poem with visual, vivid details.

Prompt 115

ABRACADABRA—I'M GONNA REACH OUT AND GRAB YA

Write a poem where you find yourself in a situation where something magical suddenly happens. Allow your imagination to create a strange scene, perhaps surreal or completely outside reality. As part of your poem, have someone tell you a secret that reveals to you something about your life. For extra credit, use at least four of the following words: citrus, prism, shallow, chickens, silk, lemons, shenanigans, chagrin, chariot, spin, prim, sin, splendid.

Prompt 116

RANT ABOUT IT

Who is driving you crazy these days? Write a rant poem based on someone who annoys you. Is a family member getting on your nerves? Is a neighbor being a pain? Does a politician have you tearing your hair out? To make sure this ends up as a poem and not just a crazed manifesto, try to avoid cliché or abstract language. Use unique and concrete images as well as active verbs, trying to balance free-flowing thought with careful crafting. Write in the form of a prose poem—a paragraph without stanzas breaks or intended line breaks.

Prompt 117

IT'S GROUNDHOG DAY!

Write a five-stanza poem where you relive the same day/scenario in each stanza, but give each stanza a slightly different outcome or perspective. For example, if you are writing about a car accident, stanza one may be about the actual accident; stanza two could explore the accident not happening; stanza three includes the accident with a different result, and so on.

Prompt 118

RINSE AND REPEAT

Write a 15 to 20 line poem in which the first word of each line is always the same. Some suggestions for words you can repeat as your first word are: praise, begin, let, understand, trust, believe, hope, assume, suppose. Address the poem to someone or something specific: lover, ex-lover, family member, friend, enemy, politician, historical figure, celebrity, a deity, nature, or something inanimate like a car, house, or computer. For extra credit, include the name of a city and a science term.

Prompt 119

MY LATEST PHOBIA

Write a poem that deals with a strange phobia (fear) that will be new to your readers. Look up odd phobias online or use one (or more) of the following: globophobia (fear of balloons), genuphobia (fear of knees), turophobia (fear of cheese), nomophobia (fear of being without a phone), alektorophobia (fear of chickens), pogonophobia (fear of beards), pediophobia (fear of dolls), ataxophobia (fear of disorder), metrophobia (fear of poetry), hylophobia (fear of trees), chorophobia (fear of dancing). Compose your poem in couplets, and don't use the words "fear," "afraid," "frightened" or "scared."

Prompt 120

PANTS ON FIRE

In Plato's *The Republic*, the philosopher suggests that poets should be banned from society because poetry can make lies appear like truths. Inspired by this notion, write a poem that makes an epic lie seem like the absolute truth. Convince your reader that smoking actually leads to longevity, that the sun revolves around the earth, or choose a personal "lie" and make it sound like the truth.

Prompt 121

LIKE A GOOD NEIGHBOR, POETRY IS THERE

Write a poem where insurance plays a major role. Maybe you're writing about earthquake insurance or how your older neighbor can no longer get car insurance because of her three accidents. Or maybe you make up a new kind of insurance—Rejection Insurance: money you receive whenever your poem is rejected. Sun Insurance: a payment you get on cloudy days. What are you afraid of losing? Would you buy insurance for that thing/person/item if you could?

Prompt 122

YOUR POEM SOUNDS VIOLET

Synesthesia is a mixing of our five senses, for example, "The grapes taste loud" or "That song sounds rectangular" or "His skin felt beige" or "The daisies smell cold." Come up with a list of five synesthesia-inspired phrases and use as many of them as you can in a poem. Write your poem in couplets and be inspired by a recent (or not-so-recent) dream.

Prompt 123

2 WAYS OF LOOKING AT RISK

Write a two-section poem. In the first section, warn the reader about something—not to chase a tornado, avoid a specific sad movie, not to fall in love, etc. Then in the second section, write the opposite sentiment, as you tell the reader to do or to consider doing the very thing you just suggested he/she shouldn't do. Use specific concrete images and similes in both sections. If you're having trouble beginning, start with, "Maybe you should…" or "Maybe you shouldn't…"

Prompt 124

LOVE AND BEAUTY
IN A TERRIBLE WORLD

Write a poem that explores beauty, love, or joy in painful, tragic, or sad times. Allow the reader to experience these opposite feelings by juxtaposing beautiful images with less pleasing ones. Maybe two people are falling in love during a hurricane, maybe someone is giving birth after just being evicted from her home. Or write in the first person about something that is inspirational to you in a not-so-perfect world.

Prompt 125

AS A CHILD, I BELIEVED I KNEW WHO LIKED BUTTER

Write a poem where you describe a specific scene from your childhood. Make sure to "show" the poem instead of "tell" it. For example, write "The underside of our chins, yellow from where we rubbed buttercups…" instead of "I liked putting buttercups on my chin." Sometimes spending a few minutes visualizing the specific details of the scene will help strengthen your poem.

Prompt 126

WARNING: AVALANCHE AREA

Write a poem where there is an avalanche of something besides snow. Maybe your poem has an avalanche of butterflies fluttering into the Amazon jungle, or perhaps you decide to take a more abstract route and have an avalanche of sadness or an avalanche of joy. Whichever you choose, use images to keep the reader engaged in new strange world.

Prompt 127

ACROSS THE UNIVERSE

Use one of the following as the first line of your poem: "Because the Earth is tilted on its axis by 23 ½ degrees..." or "Because the Sun will fade to invisibility in a billion years..." or "Because only 59% of the moon's surface is visible from Earth..." Allow your poem to be cosmic and galactic but include a few of these ordinary household items: toaster, broom, bookshelf, lamp, sofa, staircase, dryer, mirror, garage, bathtub, carpet, knick-knack, closet.

Prompt 128

STRUCTURE STRUCTURE STRUCTURE

Write a poem that employs the following constraints. When you revise your poem, you can always take out some of the constraints, but as you compose today, try to stay within these given rules: a 12 line poem with each line consisting of 8 words; each line must end in a verb (past, present, or future); each line must start with a word that begins with a vowel; somewhere in your poem include a unit of measurement, a type of fruit, a sport, and something you would find in a national park.

Prompt 129

SHORT AND SWEET

The *shadorma* is a six line poem that originated in the Spanish language. Each line has the following syllable count (from line 1 to line 6 respectively): 3/5/3/3/7/5. Write your shadorma to a specific individual and in this short poem, confess something intimate to him/her. If you are feeling inspired, write a second shadorma and make it nature-themed.

Prompt 130

BEFORE THE EARTHQUAKE, WE WERE EATING ICE CREAM AND WATCHING SEAGULLS

Write a poem about the calm before a storm. Think about times in your life when you were minding your own business and then things got out of hand. Maybe you were having a wonderful dinner before a big argument with a partner or maybe you were driving home listening to NPR then realized a tornado was moving in your direction. Use specific details to write about the calm while foreshadowing what's to come, and how you didn't know what was around the corner.

Prompt 131

INSPIRED EAVESDROPPING

Write a poem completely made up of dialogue or an overheard conversation. If you're feeling stuck, maybe go to a coffee shop, restaurant, or store and see what you overhear. You can also put on a movie (TV, Netflix, YouTube) and go into another room so that you can only catch snippets of the dialogue. Take notes on the interesting phrases you catch and use these in your poem. For extra credit, mention a recipe by name and the name of a saint.

Prompt 132

15 WAYS OF LOOKING AT A BLACK DOT

On a piece of paper, quickly make a big, black dot. Write a 12 line poem in which each line is a description of what the dot could represent. Don't mention "dot" in the poem, just describe what it could be: the eye of the cyclops, oil from my broken car, the bullet hole in granny's rocking chair… Create a poem that will intrigue and inspire your reader and don't worry about the poem making logical sense.

Prompt 133

GIVE ME ONE REASON

Compose a poem using the title "The Reasons I Became _____" (fill in the blank). Your title might read something like "The Reasons I Became a Writer," "The Reasons I Became Pissed Off," "The Reasons I Became a Loner," or "The Reasons I Became a Red-Tailed Hawk." Your poem can be practical, like why you became a poet, or your poem can be fantastical, like why you became the Grand Canyon. Consider writing your poem with no stanza breaks—just one block of text. Feel free to change the pronoun in the title to "She" or "He" or "They."

Prompt 134

BUYING SORROW, PURCHASING A CLOUD

Write a poem about buying something you cannot buy in reality. Items may include: sorrow, the ocean, a cloud, a planet, a starfish at the center of the Pacific, extra years in your life, someone's voice. The poem can be as imaginative or surreal as you need it to be. For extra credit: create a strange or unique currency to pay for these items.

Prompt 135

I WANT CANDY

Write a poem in which several types of candy play a major role. Think about using famous candy brand names: M&Ms, Three Musketeers, Almond Joy, Skittles, Starburst, etc. Or types of candy: candy corn, candy necklaces, lollipops, etc. Also consider these candy idioms: "like taking candy from a baby," "like a kid in a candy store," "eye candy," and "to candy coat." Maybe your poem will be nostalgic, about your childhood and Milk Duds or perhaps your poem will explore the way your mother always "candy-coated" every difficult situation. Sprinkle lots of sweetness (or sour lemon drops) throughout your poem.

Prompt 136

MAKE SOMETHING WONDERFUL
FROM SOMETHING TERRIBLE

William McGonagall, who died in Scotland in 1902, is widely considered the worst published poet in the history of the English language because of his melodrama and sing-songy rhymes. Choose one of McGonagall's poem titles from the following list and write a *fantastic* poem using this title: An Autumn Reverie, The Moon, The Beautiful Sun, The Destroying Angel, Lost On The Prairie, Death Of The Queen, Women's Suffrage, The Sprig Of Moss, Forget-Me-Not, The Demon Drink, Saved By Music.

Prompt 137

I'M SORRY COLLARBONE FOR MY RECKLESS MOUNTAIN BIKING

Write a poem where you apologize to your future self for some activity that you are doing today. The activity can be unhealthy, a bad habit, or just a normal activity that ends up having bad consequences for you later in life. For example, if you smoke, write an apology to your lungs. If you are afraid to travel, write an apology to your future self who never saw Rome. If you are a runner, write an apology to your future self's knees. Feel free to imagine worst-case scenarios with bizarre outcomes.

Prompt 138

SO WE BEAT ON...

Write a poem inspired by this line from F. Scott Fitzgerald's *The Great Gatsby:* "The loneliest moment in someone's life is when they are watching their whole world fall apart, and all they can do is stare blankly." For extra credit, use at least 5 of these words from the novel in your poem: ravenous, melancholy, dissolve, tender, resentment, ceaseless, menagerie, nebulous, scorn, sport, fool, ceaselessly, parties.

Prompt 139

FAIR WEATHER FRIEND

Write a poem that uses weather terminology, but whose theme is not weather related. Use some of the following weather terms: pressure, muggy, turbulence, cloudburst, gust, haze, slight chance, chill, doldrums, supersaturated, dust devil, stationary, halo, knot. For extra credit, write your poem in the form of a letter to someone who has angered you.

Prompt 140

A NOUN IS A PERSON, PLACE, OR THING

Grab the closest book and write down the first ten nouns that catch your eye. Choose your favorite of these words and write a poem where that word appears somewhere in every line. Feel free to secretly hide the word in your poem. For example, if your word is "rope," you may have one line where you write, "the he<u>ro pe</u>ers through the window" or "the sun <u>grope</u>d the sky."

Prompt 141

VIRTUAL FOREST

Technology has changed the way we speak. These words were once just "tech terms" but are now used in our daily lexicon. Write a poem specifically about nature (don't mention anything technological) and use at least six of these words or phrases: defrag, offline, online, bandwith, cache, meme, interface, hard-drive, opt out, surf the web, unplugged, spam, email, log on, hotmail, iPhone, download, upload, shareware, hacker, byte, internet connection, Facebook, Twitter, wi-fi, battery life, powercord.

Prompt 142

A CHILD'S VIEW

Write a poem about a frightening experience you had as a child. Write from an observational point of view using third person (he/she) rather than first person (I). Give the impression that the frightful experience is happening to someone else in order to maintain an objective distance. Include a rhetorical question in your poem. For extra credit, end each line of your poem with a verb.

Prompt 143

WRITE A RISPETTO

A Rispetto is a short Italian poetic form that originally had a strict syllabic meter and rhyme scheme. The simplified form consists of eight lines that are broken into two four line stanzas with each line consisting of eight syllables. If you need help coming up with a theme for your Rispetto, consider writing a poem that deals with something memorable that occurred on a holiday—Halloween, Valentine's Day, Easter, Passover, Memorial Day, etc. As a twist, don't mention the name of the holiday in the poem—simply reference it. For instance, "it was the morning of neon eggs…"

Prompt 144

WHAT'S MY LINE?

Choose a line that you like from a famous (or not so famous) poem. Now compose a poem and use the first word of the line somewhere in your first line; the second word of the line somewhere in your second line; the second word of the line somewhere in your second line, etc., until you have used each word of your chosen line. Your poem's line length will be determined by how many words are in the line you chose. For instance the line "Shall I compare thee to a summer's day" would yield a poem with 8 lines; the first line containing "shall."

Prompt 145

SHE WORKS HARD FOR THE MONEY

Write a poem about your work/job. What job do you currently hold? If you are retired, write about a typical day in your retirement or write about one of the jobs you once held. And, being a stay-at-home mom definitely counts as a job. Many of us who consider ourselves "writers" or "poets" have to work at other jobs to support ourselves. Consider this: T.S. Eliot was a banker, Maya Angelou was a cook, Carson McCullers was a waitress, William Faulkner worked in a post office, Alice Munro worked in tobacco fields. Write poem that gives your reader an inside look into your working life.

Prompt 146

A SAUCERFUL OF SECRETS

Virginia Woolf once wrote, "Every secret of a writer's soul…is written large in her works." Compose a poem that includes a real secret that you hold within yourself. You don't have to be obvious about your secret—it can be veiled, known only to you, the writer. For instance, maybe you gave up a child for adoption when you were fifteen years old—your poem could mention adoption in the second stanza—no reader would assume you are talking about yourself. Subtly, slip a real secret into your poem.

Prompt 147

THE WICKED WITCH
PICKS UP ROADSIDE LITTER

Write a poem that transforms a well-known villain in literature or movies into a hero. Surprise your readers by having this villain do a good deed. Maybe the Big Bad Wolf saves a litter of kittens he finds in the forest or perhaps Lady Macbeth volunteers at her local food bank. Could the Joker push someone out of the way of an oncoming bus? What about Lord Voldemort volunteering for a vaccine trial? Consider writing in a prose poem format.

Prompt 148

EMBEDDED BIRTHDAY POEM

Write an eight line poem that uses the date of your birthday to determine how many words per line. For instance: 11/28/1972 translates to line 1 having 1 word, line 2 having 1 word, line 3 having 2 words, etc. If your date contains zeros (02/04/1970), consider the zeros to be wildcards, and you can choose the number of words. For extra credit, reference an event that happened the year of your birth (1969 and the first moon landing).

Prompt 149

JUNK JOURNALISM NOT ALLOWED

Use some of the following jargon terms from journalism to write a poem, and for extra credit, give your poem a political theme: angle, back bench, best boy, bump, death-knock, draft, embed, flash, grip and grin, hot type, kicker, long tail, off the floor, orphan, proof, roadblock, slug, spike, tick-tock, user. If you need a first line, consider "Instead, I'm going to tell you..."

Prompt 150

A STREETCAR NAMED...

Write a poem about something or someone you are longing for. Maybe it's a new life, a new relationship, or a new president. Maybe it's a submarine sandwich or a person you have a secret crush on. Consider playing with the word "desire"—maybe repeat this word in every other line, or maybe use words that rhyme with "desire" (fire, for hire, liar, tire, etc.) throughout your poem.

Prompt 151

PUT IT IN REVERSE

Write a 12 line poem about a relationship (friendship, romantic, familial) using some or all of these words that deal with "reversing": about face, U-turn, 180 (one-eighty), flip-flop, turnaround, withdraw, reel in, backpedal, second thoughts, cold feet, null and void, revise, unsay, call off. For extra credit, write a 6 line poem using some of the above words. Now, reverse your existing poem to create the last 6 lines: line 6 becomes line 7, line 5 becomes line 8, etc. You can slightly revise these reversed lines if you need to.

Prompt 152

EXPRESS YOURSELF

Write a poem based on a ridiculous made up expression. Maybe your expression is "A rhubarb a day keeps the dentist away," "Nightmares are what holiday parties are made of," or "It's better to giggle than to recite." You can play with this expression throughout your poem (or keep creating more of them) or title your poem with this expression and write a poem that shows the strange expression coming to life.

Prompt 153

A MAGICAL MYSTERY TOUR

Write a poem inspired by one of these Beatles' song titles: *Come Together, A Day in the Life, Blackbird, Penny Lane, I Am the Walrus, My Guitar Gently Weeps, She Loves You, Paperback Writer, Revolution, Back in the USSR, Baby You're a Rich Man.* To continue the nod to the Beatles, include at least 5 of the following words: beetle, imagine, Ringo, fab four, mop tops, apple, vinyl records, London, Liverpool, British invasion, Lucy, sky, diamonds, or submarine (extra credit if it's yellow).

Prompt 154

PEACH, WASTELAND, TROUSERS, CATS

Grab the nearest book or magazine and write down 14 random words. Now write a 14-line poem in which one word is used in each line until you have used all the words. Maybe write in the form of a sonnet, using end-rhymes, if you would like the challenge of using a specific form. For extra credit, have your title subtly refer to the name of the book or magazine that you used.

Prompt 155

A WORLD OF POSSIBILITY

For the title of your poem, complete the following: "What If_____?" and structure your poem so that it contains 3 stanzas of any length in which you explore your "what if." In the first stanza, mention a famous poet and a type of flower or plant. In the second stanza, mention the title of a book and a word that starts with "z." In the final stanza, reference a musical instrument and use a simile: "_____ is like _____."

Prompt 156

AMERICAN SENTENCES

The poet Allen Ginsberg created a variation of the Haiku—rather than dividing the 17 syllable form into 3 lines, he wrote a single sentence consisting of 17 syllables, aptly named "American Sentence." Here is one of Ginsberg's "sentences": "Crescent moon, girls chatter at twilight on the bus ride to Ankara." Try writing 4 or 5 "American Sentences" using only 17 syllables per line and keeping the flavor of the Haiku—a simple moment observing something in nature.

Prompt 157

PLEASE BE MY SUGAR PLUM
AND BABY DOLL

Write a poem using words that are considered sentimental, but create a tone that is sarcastic, edgy, or ironic. Use these "sappy" words in a surprising way to create an interesting contrast in your poem. Is it possible to describe climate change as "lovely" or "heartfelt" using irony? What about a dictator being referred to as "sweetie pie"? Here is a list of sentimental words to use (or come up with some of your own): dearest, melody, sunshine, sugar, twinkle, precious, wonderful, cuddle, honey, wistful, yearning, snuggle, cutie.

Prompt 158

DREAMWEAVER

Quickly jot down four things you saw happen the last few days and four specific memories that happened to you as a teenager/young adult. Write a dream poem where you weave all eight of these memories together in a poem. Because it's a dream, remember that chronological order doesn't matter—you can mold or change the narrative as needed, and things can disappear or reappear as needed. Don't worry about being logical—let your subconscious speak.

Prompt 159

ALL IN GOOD TIME,
MY LITTLE PRETTY

The book, *Wicked,* written by Gregory Maguire, considers the story of *The Wizard of Oz*, but from the Wicked Witch's perspective. Think of a character who is either loved or hated, and write a poem from the opposite perspective. For example, maybe Captain Hook is a misunderstood failed costume designer who always wanted to live a flamboyant lifestyle, but his dad wanted him to be a pirate. Or maybe Gandalf from *Lord of the Rings* isn't actually predicting doom and destruction, but creating it. Feel free to choose the character from a book, movie, cartoon, or TV show.

Prompt 160

HOLLY HOLY DREAM

Write a poem that uses the following word pairs that look and/or sound alike: angle/angel; sole/soul; bread/bred; wonder/wander; presence/presents; suit/suite; quiet/quite; orchard/orchid; finance/fiancé; holy/holly; chord/cord; price/prize. Choose at least 6 of these word pairs (or more!) to use in your poem. These word pairs do not need to appear on the same line, but if you are in the mood for a challenge today, try placing the pair in the same line: "She wonders how much he will wander beyond their circumference…"

Prompt 161

I DON'T HAVE A CLUE

Remember playing the board game Clue? You had to solve a mystery of a homicide by a certain person, in a certain room, with a certain weapon. Winning answers might read something like, "Colonel Mustard in the ballroom with a candlestick." As a twist on the Clue game, write a poem that includes a character from Clue: Professor Plum, Mrs. White, Miss Scarlet; a room: kitchen, hallway, dining room; and an item: pipe, rope, knife. Your poem can be about any topic, but should include these subtle embedded references to the game of Clue. If you want, include the word "clue" somewhere in your poem.

Prompt 162

SHE'S GOT BETTE DAVIS THIGHS

Write a poem that mentions a misheard song lyric. For instance, some people have misheard the Bee Gees' "Staying Alive" as "Steak and a Knife" or "Saying a Lie." Others have mistaken this lyric from "Dancing Queen": "feel the beat from the tangerine" instead of "feel the beat from the tambourine." Some have misheard one of Elton John's lyrics: "hold me closer, Tony Danza" instead of "hold me closer, tiny dancer." Think about lyrics you haven't heard correctly, and have fun with this prompt!

Prompt 163

ALWAYS, TRULY, YOURS

Write a poem in the form of a letter to someone who has died. You can begin with "Dear _____," or just jump into the poem by addressing the person by name. Maybe the individual is a friend or relative, maybe someone famous you have never met. Use the poem as a device to connect present with past using images to share what you are feeling. End the poem with something you wish the person would have known when s/he was alive (for instance, you wish your grandmother had known your children).

Prompt 164

CLOTHES MAKE THE POET

Write a poem in which clothing takes a starring role. Maybe in your poem a wedding dress will figure prominently or a precious hand-me-down item, an old bra, a negligee, a suit or dress for a burial, some cowboy boots, a child's first holiday outfit, a clothing item from a deceased loved one, etc. Pick an item of clothing that carries some spark and emotion for you as this will give your poem an added vitality and immediacy.

Prompt 165

HOW TO MAKE CHANGE
AND INFLUENCE PEEPHOLES

Write a poem where you reference a book or movie that doesn't exist. You can create a more serious title like *Climate Change for a World Who Doesn't Care* or a sillier title like *How To Wear Cowboy Boots If You Live in the City.* Make up several pretend books or movies and use them throughout the poem. For extra credit, mention an exotic animal, a street name, and a type of hat.

Prompt 166

TAKE ME HOME, COUNTRY ROADS

Wallace Stegner wrote, "I may not know who I am, but I know where I'm from." Where are you from? What geographical place do you identify as your point of origin? Write a poem that explores where you are from. If you grew up in Muddy Creek, West Virginia, write a poem where this locale takes front and center stage. Make your hometown location come alive for your readers—what makes Muddy Creek special? What happened there? What's it look like? What are its pros and cons? What part of Muddy Creek do you still embody? Include the name of where you are from in the title of your poem.

Prompt 167

"ALTERNATIVE FACTS" OR TWO LIES AND ONE TRUTH

Write a poem in which you incorporate two outlandish lies. These "lies" can be untruths about you (the poet). For example, "When I first saw the great pyramid..." although you have never visited Egypt. Or these "lies" can be historical or contemporary—"The South won the Civil War." Also incorporate one revealing truth about yourself—"The day I was arrested..." Allow the reader to determine what is true or false without being self-conscious.

Prompt 168

DEAR COFFEE,
I WISH YOU WERE VODKA

Write a poem where you wish something in everyday life was either different or another color. Maybe you wish the moon was mauve or that your toaster was really a drummer named Danny. Throughout your poem, show an image, then wish that image were something else. Allow the poem to be absurd in places, letting your imagination stretch into the bizarre.

Prompt 169

LUCKY 7

Write a poem where every line has only seven words. The poem can be about any topic, but think about what comes to mind when you think of the word "seven" (7-11, 7Up, Seven Sisters, Seven Dwarves, Seven Deadly Sins, etc.), and maybe let one of those topics (or several) inform your poem. For an opening consider using, "One way to. . ." For extra credit, slip in a few words that rhyme or slant rhyme with seven: heaven, leaven, eleven, even, raven, etc.

Prompt 170

WHAT IF

Write a poem in which each line begins with the phrase "What if…" Your "what if" lines can follow a logical flow, such as: *What if I never married you / What if I only lived out of a backpack…* Or, your poem can list a series of "what if" questions that might have no obvious connection, such as: *What if I saw Elvis at the pizza place / What if I painted my kitchen black…* As you compose your poem and continuously ask yourself "what if," let your imagination run wild. Aim for at least 12 lines, and when you revise, see what happens to your poem if you take out the "What if" phrases.

Prompt 171

YOUR BODY IS A WONDERLAND

Here are some strange facts about the body: it is physically impossible for you to lick your elbow; like fingerprints, everyone's tongue print is different; your heart beats over 100,000 times a day; women blink nearly twice as often as men; the longest bout of hiccups lasted nearly 69 years; most of the dust particles in your house are dead skin. Write a poem that includes one or more of these facts, or write a poem about a strange fact that has to do with your own body.

Prompt 172

I WAS ARRESTED FOR INDECENT EXPOSURE IN CHURCH!

Write a poem in first person in which you convincingly convey to your reader something scandalous that is, in reality, not true. Go big with this! Make up something quite outlandish that you would never really have done, and write a poem that chronicles the event as if it happened. Maybe you bungee jumped off of the Space Needle or maybe you were fired from your job because of a prank that went wrong or maybe…

Prompt 173

TEENY TINY

Write a poem that is between 8 and 12 lines. Limit each line length to five words or less. Limit each word to five letters or less. Basically, this will be a poem consisting only of small words. In order to create an interesting contrast in your poem, choose a theme that is very large—the universe, the ocean, a redwood forest, dinosaurs, whales, the pyramids, a cruise ship, an extra-large pizza, etc. As a twist, use a very large word in your title consisting of at least 10 or more letters.

Prompt 174

SCORE A GOAL

Take some time to think about your current list of goals in your life. Make a list of very practical goals—need to fix the gate, clean the attic, extend the vegetable garden, etc. Now, make a list of pie-in-the-sky goals, holding nothing back on your fantastical wishes—want to spend eight weeks in Japan, start a million dollar business, adopt one hundred homeless pets, etc. Choose one goal/wish from each list and use them in a poem.

Prompt 175

SHORT SHORT STORY

For this prompt, compose a short prose poem that tells a narrative story. Maybe you have recently had an interesting experience that could be encapsulated in a few lines or perhaps you just heard about someone's adventure or mishap that would make a good short story in prose poem format. Include the following "story" elements: character(s), rising action, climax, falling action, and resolution. Try to keep your prose poem under 100 words.

Prompt 176

FOR SALE: BAZOOKA BUBBLE GUM FROM 1968

Write a poem using some of the following odd "for sale" items that have been found on Craigslist: turquoise air, friend of Barbie, fertile duck eggs, 1970's Jesus statue, a reclaimed life, retired queen, awesome tiki gods, human-sized hamster wheel, full-size Amish figures made of wax, chicken diapers, a sofa made of stones, a heart-shaped potato, a mural made of Pop Tarts. Use at least four of the items mentioned above within your poem. For extra credit, give your poem a political theme.

Prompt 177

THE JOKE IS ON YOU

Write a poem that initially gives the impression that it is going to be a joke, that something funny is going to take place. As a twist, allow the poem to travel into sad or dark topics so that the reader is surprised where the poem ends up. If you're having trouble beginning, maybe start with the familiar first line of a traditional joke: "A _____ and a _____walk into a bar..." or "Why did the _____cross the road?" or "Knock, Knock...".

Prompt 178

WITH A LITTLE HELP FROM ROBERT HASS

In first line of "Meditations at Lagunitas," Robert Hass writes, "All the new thinking is about loss." Taking a nod from Robert Hass, begin a poem with the line: "All the old thinking is about _____ "(fill in the blank). Your word could be an abstract word like distress or bliss, or it could be a concrete noun like department stores or newspapers. Feel free to include an epigraph in your poem, "After Robert Hass" acknowledging your inspiration.

Prompt 179

THE NUMBERS DON'T LIE

Write a 10-line poem in which each line has ten syllables. Try to include words or images that have to do with math, money, dates, or anything that includes numbers (telephone numbers, addresses, zip codes, etc.) If you need an opening line, begin the poem with one of the following, "On a scale of one to ten…" or "Because the numbers say…" or "It doesn't add up…"

Prompt 180

IF YOU GOT THE NOTION

A recent study finds that there are 27 human emotions that we all experience at various times. Compose a poem consisting of at least 4 stanzas (or more). In each stanza personify a different emotion: "today my anger took me for a walk and kept jerking on my collar…" or "his envy is throwing darts at my back…" Here are a few of the less common emotional states that the study identifies: awkwardness, triumph, nostalgia, craving, entrancement, empathetic pain, aesthetic appreciation, boredom.

Prompt 181

ABC, EASY AS 123

Write an abecedarian poem—a poem in which the first letter of each line begins with a letter of the alphabet (starting with "a" then "b" then "c," etc.). Your poem can be about any topic you wish, but consider writing about things that are in alphabetical order, such as dictionaries, phone books, card catalogs, names on a war memorial, a well-organized spice rack, etc.

Prompt 182

AFTERNOON DELIGHT

Write a poem that shows delight in something common or a small detail in life. Maybe you are delighted by a feather or leaf that keeps being lifted by the wind. Or maybe it's that the barista at Starbucks put a heart by your name. Focus on all the details and specifics around the small thing you choose. For extra credit, compose your poem in three line stanzas.

Prompt 183

DON'T BRING UP POLITICS OR RELIGION

For today's poem, break the famous rule that people should avoid politics and religion when engaging in polite discourse. Write a poem that is unabashedly political or religious. Don't hold back your opinions, but rather, let them flow out unedited. Write about a politician or political situation that really upsets you, or write about a politician whom you love. Write about what irks you regarding your family's long-held religious beliefs, or write about a powerful mystical experience you once had.

Prompt 184

WRITE YOUR OWN RULES

Write a fourteen-line poem that is a variation on the sonnet. Look up the rules for both an English and Italian sonnet and riff on one of those forms in a creative way. Change up the rhyme scheme or do away with it. Make a rule for how many words are allowed per line or maybe each line must start with a noun. Keep the fourteen line structure, but get inventive with the rest of the form by creating at least three new rules. For extra credit, avoid referencing anything to do with "love" or relationships in your sonnet.

Prompt 185

WERE YOU A PHILATELIST AS A CHILD?

Think back to a time in your life or in childhood when you enjoyed collecting something. Maybe you collected stamps, comic books, baseball cards or had a windowsill filled with dachshund figurines. Or maybe you had a rock tumbler, and you walked your streets looking for anything shiny to polish. Write a poem where the speaker is obsessed with his/her collection. Allow the collected objects to appear and reappear in the poem as much as possible.

Prompt 186

THERE COULD BE TOURISTS

Write a poem about tourists walking through a place where there aren't usually tourists. Maybe you find a man in a Hawaiian shirt in your bathroom or a family in bathing suits and a beach umbrella in the cereal aisle of your grocery store. Write a poem that includes what they discover in these normal places. Do they buy a souvenir? Take a selfie? Stand on your toilet and look at the view? Allow your poem to be as humorous or strange as needed.

Prompt 187

TO THE MOON AND BACK!

Write a poem where you are about to undertake a journey to an unusual destination. Consider all the impossible places you can't visit, and imagine traveling to one. Perhaps, you want to travel to a secret basement in the White House or to a cloud. Include in the poem what you'll pack and what you'll leave home. Consider beginning your poem, "When I leave for _____, I'll bring…"

Prompt 188

DOUBLE, DOUBLE, TOIL AND TROUBLE

Write a poem in the form of a spell. Include ingredients that most likely wouldn't be used in a traditional spell, such as a tie-tack, the color blue, a coffee thermos, a tiara, an avocado, etc. Begin by making a quick list of these "non-spell ingredients" and then decide who or what you are bewitching. Consider titling your poem: "Spell For _____. " For extra credit, include the name of a movie star or singer you had a crush on as a teenager.

Prompt 189

BOB MARLEY AND JAMMIN'
WITH LITTLE BIRDS

Write a poem while listening to a specific style of music: jazz, hip-hop, blues, country, reggae, opera, heavy metal, classical, swing, etc. As you listen to the music, begin writing without editing yourself—jot down a list of the images and phrases that are inspired by the music, no matter how odd or disjointed they may seem. Maybe country music has you seeing barns, mountains, and grandma's cherry pie, while heavy metal has you envisioning the apocalypse and zombies. Once you have a list of images and phrases, use them to compose your poem.

Prompt 190

LONG-ARM OF THE LAWFUL POET

Poet Ellen Bass talks about "long-arm poems" that reach out and draw in many different topics, feelings, words, time periods, pop-culture references, etc. Make a list of twenty-five things that do not seem to have a lot in common (ballet, holding an axe as a child, moray eels, a loved one dying, trying to choose a paint color for the walls, etc.). Now write a poem where you bring in as many as those images and words as possible.

Prompt 191

UPTIGHT OUTTA SIGHT

The culture of the 1960s developed some fantastic slang words. For today's prompt, embed some of these terms in your poem in a subtle way. For instance the term "far out" can become "my grandma's birthplace was far out of town..." and "threads" (a term for clothes) can be embedded "the red threads of my anger..." Here are some 60s words to embed in your poem: gnarly, cool, fuzz, square, dough, dig it, hip, grass, hang loose, fox, chick, blast, pad, dude, boss, neat, rap, shades, score, wicked, later, loaded.

Prompt 192

STAR STRUCK

Write a poem that incorporates the following astronomical terms, but don't write about stars, space, or astronomy. Instead, write a poem about a relationship in your life—spouse, parent, child, friend, coworker, etc. The poem can be either positive or negative in terms of the relationship and should include some of the following astronomical terms: black hole, blue moon, eclipse, constellation, galaxy, light-year, phase, opposition, sunspot, twilight, zodiac.

Prompt 193

SELF-PORTRAIT WITH BEYONCE

Write a self-portrait poem with a favorite artist or musician. Maybe it's "Self Portrait with Andy Warhol" where you collect Campbell's soup cans together. Or perhaps, it's "Self-Portrait with the Beatles" where you nap in their Yellow Submarine. Choose an artist or musician who inspires you, and for extra credit, use titles of his/her work or songs in your poem.

Prompt 194

TAKE A STAND

Write a poem in which your stand on an issue is the central theme. The issue can be anything from switching your breakfast routine from granola to eggs or why global climate change is an immediate threat. Whether your "issue" is small and personal (breakfast) or is social/political (climate change), compose a poem that strongly takes a stand (eggs are *better* than granola or climate change *will impact* US coastal cities). Also include the following words: resonate, split, pale, frayed, extra, circle, study.

Prompt 195

HEADLINERS

Take a moment to scan a few of today's headlines and find a story that really irks you and gets you irritated. Title the poem by using a creative variation of the headline title. Create irregular stanzas and odd line breaks, allowing your poem to have a life of its own as you write quickly—try not to edit yourself, but tap into your subconscious. Be ok with images or phrases that don't make logical sense. Write until your irritation has been expressed and only lightly revise your poem.

Prompt 196

THE OCCASIONAL POEM

Write a poem that begins "Occasionally, we stretch _____ …" and fill in the blank with a surprising image. Some ideas might include *stars, each other*, *the sorrow, time and the hands of a clock*. You can also change the verb "stretch" to another verb such as "Occasionally, we *tango* with the stock market" or "Occasionally, we misunderstand the landscape." Your poem can be about any topic, and for extra credit, create several sentences in this format and use them throughout the poem.

Prompt 197

WHY DO TODAY
WHAT YOU CAN DO TOMORROW?

All of us are procrastinators at some point in our lives—putting off something until it becomes a sort of monster at our backs, waking us up at 2 a.m. as we toss and turn, promising ourselves we'll do "it" when we wake in the morning. Think about something in your life that you are currently putting off doing—getting your finances in order, putting a new roof on your house, getting the oil changed in your car, writing an email to someone, etc. Use this current thing hanging over your head as the main subject of your poem, and explore your mental block when it comes to getting this thing done.

Prompt 198

ZEUS, MOLDY CHEDDAR, AND THE TANGO

Write a poem that mentions each of the following (in any order): a character from Greek/Roman mythology, something you might find in a barn, the oldest item currently in your refrigerator, your least favorite animal or insect, a type of dance, something that is in the form of a circle, the first name of a famous poet, a number consisting of at least three digits, the cause of the last time that you cried, and an over-the-counter medicine. Don't edit or overthink your responses.

Prompt 199

I WASN'T THERE

Choose an event at which you were not present. This event can be completely fictitious (I wasn't present when the moon and sun collided) or the event can be historic (I wasn't present when Cleopatra kissed Julius Caesar) or it can be an actual event (I wasn't present when my father died). Write a poem that plays with the implications of not being present for a certain event. Your poem can be fanciful—"She wasn't there when the moon hit the sun / but she dreams about a big bang…" or your poem can be serious—"I made it to my father's hospital room / and the sheets were already piled on the floor…"

Prompt 200

MAD, BAD, AND DANGEROUS IN PLAID

Use at least one of these "worst romance novel titles" in a poem: *The Bull Rider's Christmas Baby, Held Captive By The Cavemen, Jungle Freakin' Bride, The Very Virile Viking, I Knocked Up Satan's Daughter*. In keeping with the theme of "romance," consider writing about the day to day realities of a relationship or marriage—the frustrations, the occasional boredom, the silly arguments over something like cat litter or dirty dishes, how the predictable habits of a significant other can drive you crazy.

Prompt 201

SUGAR, AH HONEY HONEY

Write a poem where you describe an emotion (sadness, joy, love, resentment, grief, etc.) through words associated with baking. Use at least seven of these words in your poem: flour, blend, brownie, cake, cookie cutter, measure, butter, dissolve, dust, sugar, jelly-roll pan, melt, mix, nonstick, oven, pumpernickel, brown sugar, knead, stir, zest.

Prompt 202

THERE ARE PLENTY OF FISH IN THE SEA

Compose a poem using as many of these terms from fishing as you can (extra credit for using all of the terms), but don't write about the act of fishing. Consider writing about a relationship or a recent event in your life. Use the fishing words in a creative way, playing on their multiple meanings. Here are your terms: bait, drift, strike, backlash, angle, hook, bobbing, lure, leader, fly, casting, bite, net, spin, line, snag, trace.

Prompt 203

X MARKS THE SPOT

Write a poem in which you find a map that leads to a treasure. To find what your "treasure" is, pick up the nearest book, go to page 22, and point to the first concrete noun you see. That noun is what you discover in the poem. If you are feeling stuck, write the poem as a dream. For extra credit, reference books, movies, or characters that deal with treasure hunting: Tom Sawyer, Huck Finn, Indiana Jones, Laura Croft, Pirates of the Caribbean, etc.

Prompt 204

IT'S A PITY

When was the last time you gave yourself a "pity party?" Go back to an event that led you to feel truly sorry for yourself (either justified or unjustified). How were you wronged? Who wronged you? How did it feel in detail? Use this "pity party" in today's poem and include the following: a type of house plant, a child's toy, and an item found in a garage.

Prompt 205

GRUMPY, HAPPY, DOPEY...

Write a poem that includes your answer to one of these "most popular" Google searches: *Why are manhole covers round? Who are the seven dwarves? What are rolled oats? Where do hummingbirds sleep? Where's my refund? What time is sunset? Why were cornflakes invented? Why am I so tired? Is Europe a country? Does the moon rotate? Can dogs eat bananas? Are koalas really bears?* When you answer one or more of these questions in your poem, make your answer creative—maybe hummingbirds sleep inside of mailboxes or on moonbeams.

Prompt 206

THAT GOLD MINE IS MINE

The following is a list of words that have multiple meanings: *bank, club, current, prune, patient, novel, file, light, draft, pound, mine, stamp, stern, kid, loom, head, bark, pupil, fly.* Choose at least seven words from this list (or think up your own multiple meaning words), and use each word twice in your poem illustrating two different meanings of the word. For instance, one line might be "my money is in the bank…" while later on in your poem, another line might read "on the river's bank…"

Prompt 207

I TAKE THAT BACK!

A "Palinode" is a little-known poetic form that consists of a poem that "takes back" or retracts the sentiment expressed in a previous poem that you have written. For instance, maybe in the past you wrote a love poem about your significant other, but now you are no longer together or maybe you once wrote a poem that embarrasses you and you want to "take back" those feelings you expressed. Think about a poem you have previously written (recently or a long time ago) and, if possible, find that poem and write a retraction of it. If you find a love poem that is no longer applicable, write a poem that explains why the feelings of love have since disappeared.

Prompt 208

ICKY YUCKY BLAH POEM

Write a poem that incorporates as many of these "ugliest sounding words in the English language" as you can: *gurgle, curd, chunky, bulbous, munch, clogged, jowls, slurp, quark, honk, crotch, juror, sap, gripe, angst, gob, funk, jukebox, crackpot, bulge, Sputnik*. For extra credit, work in three or four of these most pleasant sounding words: *silence, chimes, mist, murmuring, golden, wisteria, Shenandoah, lullaby*.

Prompt 209

THE ANGELS WANT TO WEAR MY RED SHOES

Write a poem where an angel or devil interacts with you in a poem. Maybe it's a loved one returning to tell you something they've learned in heaven or maybe there's a small devil living in a mouse hole near your kitchen pantry. Consider different types of angels and devils, such as the Los Angeles Angels, Dirt Devil vacuum, deviled ham, guardian angels, etc. to add a bit more playfulness to your poem. For extra credit, include an item of clothing and allow the angel or devil to wear it.

Prompt 210

@#$%^&*()!

Write a poem that incorporates symbols or made-up equations: #, @, $, *, %, +, *~X=poem/2+image*. Feel free to use the symbols in the poem in your own unique (and possibly unusual) way, such as "Sometimes the $$$ just doesn't +." See how using symbols changes what and how you are writing. Do you become more experimental in your work? If you're looking for an opening line try, "The $ tears my…"

Prompt 211

WHY DO WE KEEP WRITING POEMS?

Think of a "why" question (why is the sky blue, why can't I find love, why I love/dislike the color yellow, etc.) and answer it in multiple, surprising, and beautiful ways. Have each line of your poem consist of one of the answers. Try for at least ten different answers. For extra credit, begin each line with the word, "Because…" Consider using your "why" question as the title of the poem.

Prompt 212

IMAGINARY GARDENS WITH REAL TOADS

Write a poem that includes a famous poet doing something unpoetic and unexpected. Maybe there will be a quick mention of Emily Dickinson writing trashy romance novels or Robert Frost using Lysol to clean his toilet. Consider writing this poem as a "defense of poetry"—address why poetry is important within our society, how symbols and images can convey important truths, or perhaps take the devil's advocate route, and write a poem that rants why poetry isn't really important. For some added insight, go online and read Marianne Moore's poem, *Poetry*, which addresses the topic of poetry's place in the world.

Prompt 213

BRAVE HEART

Think about a time when you were forced to be courageous and create a poem with elements of that experience. Avoid using the words "courage," "bravery," "fearless," or "daring." Incorporate at least five of the following words: wobble, puzzle, hole, pretend, factual, mirror, fiction, distant, wall, cards, weather. End your poem with a question.

Prompt 214

ONCE UPON A TIME

Use one of the following lesser known fairytale titles in your poem. Don't worry about looking up the details of the story—simply be inspired by the title itself and perhaps use it as the title of your poem. Choose one of the following: "The Flea," "The Wonderful Birch," "The Dog and the Sparrow," "The She-Bear," "The Maiden with the Rose on Her Forehead," "The Water of Life," "The Crumbs on the Table," "The Goose Girl at the Well," "The Bright Sun Brings it to Light." Perhaps your poem will tell its own version of the fairytale, or perhaps your poem will relate the title to something in your life.

Prompt 215

DO YOU BELIEVE IN MAGIC?

Write a poem about a relationship (new lover, marriage, friendship ending, mother/father, or death of a parent, etc.) that includes these terms from magic: abracadabra, presto, hocus pocus, fairy dust, wand, sleight of hand, misdirection, illusion, parlor trick, cabinet escape, bullet catch. For extra credit, include one of these magicians (or magician duos) in your poem: Houdini, David Copperfield, Penn & Teller, David Blaine, or Shin Lim.

Prompt 216

EXPLORE YOUR BAD NATURE

Choose one of the following inspirational quotes about nature, and in your poem, disagree with the sentiments of the quote: "I never saw a discontented tree" (John Muir); "The best thing one can do when it is raining is to let it rain" (H.W. Longfellow); "Deep in their roots, all flowers keep the light" (Theodore Roethke). Your poem might be about the discontented tree in your neighbor's yard that has been over-pruned, or perhaps your poem might rage against the rain.

Prompt 217

DIFFERENT DAY

Write a poem about something you would never write about (or want to write about). For instance if you usually write nature poems, write a poem that deals with the inner city. Compose your poem differently—if you normally write short lines, make a point to write in long lines across the page, and if you usually type your poems on a computer, write this poem on paper with a pen or pencil. If you normally write at your desk, sit somewhere else to write. Try to do as many things differently today as you can, and see what happens.

Prompt 218

WRITING ABOUT WRITING

Stephen King explains his writing routine: "I have a glass of water or I have a cup of tea. I have my vitamin pill; I have my music; I have my same seat; and the papers are all arranged in the same places." Write a poem that gives your reader insight into your writing routine—maybe you write in bed with a cup of cocoa, soft lighting, listening to jazz or maybe you write in a bathtub with candles, wine, and a collection of Elizabeth Bishop poems for inspiration. Perhaps you snatch moments of quick writing on the city bus in the evening. Write a poem about the setting of *your* specific writing routine.

Prompt 219

FRANKLY, MY DEAR,
I DON'T GIVE A DAMN

Make a quick list of the following: two foods you ate last night for dinner, the topic of your last Facebook post or tweet or text, two foreign words or phrases, three adjectives you associate with "deadline," and one memorable movie line. Now use this list in a ten to fifteen line poem. For extra credit, write this poem without punctuation as one continuous and very long sentence.

Prompt 220

RIKKI DON'T LOSE THAT NUMBER

Who was the last person or organization or business to call you or text you on your phone? Write a poem to this person or organization and directly address him/her/they/it as you write. Maybe your child or spouse has just texted you or maybe the bank has just called to say that there are suspicious withdrawals from your checking account. Have you ever written a poem that directly addresses a loved one? Have you ever written a poem directly addressing a collections agency? Consider beginning your poem with, "When I saw it was you…"

Prompt 221

WHEN WE WERE YOUNG

Write a poem where you write about an event (personal or national) that includes details of your childhood. Did you have SPAM for dinner, drink Fresca or Orange Crush, ride without seatbelts while your parents smoked in the front seat? Write a poem in first or third person where you show the differences of then and now while you explore an event—maybe the space walk, maybe Bobby Kennedy or Ronald Reagan being shot, or some other memory that resonates with you.

Prompt 222

WAIT, WHO SENT THIS?

A safety pin. A lock of hair. A bandaid. A piece of broken glass. What do you not expect to find in an envelope that has been sent to you? Write a poem where you receive something very strange in an envelope. Include details, like where the envelope was sent from, is the address handwritten or typed, what sort of stamp is on it, etc. For extra credit, add an element of mystery by having the speaker try to figure out who sent her/him this odd item.

Prompt 223

BIRD IS THE WORD

Write a poem from the perspective of a specific kind of bird, like a blue heron, hawk, sparrow, hummingbird, seagull, etc. Write in the first person as though the bird is speaking, but don't tell your readers directly that the poem is actually in the voice of a bird. You might begin, "When I look down on the beach…" or "When I sit in the moonlight…" Include details of what the landscape looks like from the sky, from a nest, from a treetop, etc. Consider listening to a bird-themed song before you begin: *Free Bird, Fly Like An Eagle, When Doves Cry, Blackbird, Hummingbird, Rockin' Robin,* etc.

Prompt 224

WHEN HAIKU BECOMES UKIAH

Reverse the standard Haiku form (a three line poem consisting of five, seven, and five syllables respectively) and write a three line poem that is seven syllables (first line), five syllables (second line), and seven syllables (third line). Choose a theme unrelated to nature (the usual Haiku topic): graffiti on an overpass, a presidential election, Walmart, an argument, housework, a visit to the dentist, etc. Write at least four of these reverse Haiku, each with a different non-nature theme.

Prompt 225

DEAR DADA

Artist Max Ernst was one of the pioneers of the Dada and Surrealism movements. Be inspired by some of his painting titles (use the titles directly in your poem, or just use a word or two from the title, or be inspired in a surreal way): the fireside angel, the eye of silence, birth of a galaxy, everyone here speaks Latin, murdering airplane, the wavering woman, two children are threatened by a nightingale, dream and revolution, totem and taboo. Note: the painting titles are intentionally uncapped and not italicized.

Prompt 226

A TRIBUTE TO AESOP

Fables are stories that usually involve animals as characters which point out both good and bad behavior in the human world. Inspired by the meaning of fables, write a poem in which an animal (or animals) gives you (or the poem's speaker) a certain insight. Maybe in your poem the speaker is driving in her/his car feeling defeated when suddenly a bald eagle flies across the road, giving the speaker a sudden insight on strength. Maybe your pet's behavior offers you a clue as you work to solve ·a problem. Include the animal in your title.

Prompt 227

ONE DAY THE UNIVERSE WILL LOVE _____ (INSERT YOUR NAME HERE)

Poet Roger Reeves wrote a poem called "Some Day You'll Love Roger Reeves." Several years later, Ocean Vuong, inspired by Reeves, wrote his poem, "Some Day You'll Love Ocean Vuong." Write a poem where your first or last name either appears in the title or first/last line of the poem. Let the poem tell you some things you need to know in your current situation, or let the poem show you images that have been important throughout your life. Feel free to refer to or address yourself in the poem as needed. You can make this poem very personal and tweak the title in whatever way you want.

Prompt 228

DOWN HOME COMFORT

Create a quick list of seven items that evoke within you a feeling of comfort, warmth, being taken care of. Perhaps this list will include a cheesy pasta dish or a certain soft blanket or a piece of jewelry given to you by a beloved grandma or aunt. Now, think of a recent situation in which you felt very uncomfortable. Write a poem about your discomfort and include at least five items from your "comfort list."

Prompt 229

THE EXCELLENT AND THE HORRIBLE

Write a poem that uses the title of a well-respected novel and the title of a very bad movie. Here are possible novel titles to choose: *To Kill a Mockingbird, Wuthering Heights, The Great Gatsby, The Handmaid's Tale, Beloved, The Scarlet Letter, Of Mice and Men*. And here are some horrible movies: *Killer Tomatoes Eat France; Santa with Muscles; Help! I'm a Fish; Cannibal Women in the Avocado Jungle of Death; Hollywood Chainsaw Hookers; Space Zombie Bingo; Rabid Grannies*. Mention a good novel and a bad movie, and compose your poem in couplets.

Prompt 230

IT TAKES TWO, BABY

Write a poem where an incredibly famous couple does some pretty boring, regular stuff. When considering that activity the couple may do, consider what they are known for and try to put a "spin" on that activity. Maybe Adam and Eve bake an apple pie, Romeo and Juliet organize a family potluck, or Marilyn Monroe and Joe DiMaggio play catch in their backyard. Some couples to consider: Antony & Cleopatra, Ricky & Lucy, Bert & Ernie, Amelia Earhart & George Putnam, Fred & Daphne, or John & Yoko.

Prompt 231

THE DEEP REFLECTIONS OF DAFFY DUCK

Write a poem in the form of a journal entry made by a famous fictional character from cartoons, books, TV, movies, etc. Structure your poem in the way that you envision the lines in a handwritten journal. Perhaps your poem will be a prose poem—one solid block of words. Maybe your poem will have long lines and irregular stanza breaks. Explore the heartfelt (or humorous) topics that your chosen character might write about. What would Sherlock Holmes ponder? What might Wonder Woman be angry about? Try getting into the mind of this character, and then allow yourself to write without much editing.

Prompt 232

A POET'S BEST FRIEND

Edgar Allan Poe is said to have always written with his pet cat on his shoulder. Write a poem about a beloved (or not so beloved) animal in your life. Maybe your favorite pet companion is a deceased beagle or you had a special connection to a horse as a child. Maybe your grandmother had a white cat who always scratched you. As you write about this animal in your life, try to end each line of your poem with "ing" words: barking, sleeping, ring, ceiling, evening, etc. Aim for at least twelve lines.

Prompt 233

ELEANOR ROOSEVELT ONCE TOLD ME...

For this prompt, choose four historic or famous figures and allow each one to tell you something important. Each figure's words to you will form a stanza of your poem. For instance, your first stanza might begin, "Joan of Arc advised..." and your second stanza might begin, "David Bowie said..." Think about which people you would like to invite into your poem, and imagine what each one might say specifically to you. Does Albert Einstein have some important info to whisper in your ear? Would Betty White give you insight into aging? Feel free to expand your poem to more than four stanzas.

Prompt 234

LIVIN' IN THE FUTURE

Think about any recent premonitions or intuitive feelings you have had. Write a few of these "predictions" in a list and choose one to use as the theme for today's poem. Maybe your intuition is telling you there might be a future presidential impeachment or maybe you sense that your newly married daughter is pregnant or perhaps you feel that an earthquake is about to occur in your area. Take a moment to listen to your intuitive side, and write your poem about a future event that might occur.

Prompt 235

A HUGE TRIBUTE TO PAPERCLIPS!

Pablo Neruda has a collection of poems called "Odes to Common Things" in which he pays tribute and homage to everyday items. In the spirit of an ode (tribute, honor, homage), write a poem that shows your gratitude and respect for a "common thing" in your household. Neruda wrote about ironing, cats, tomatoes, garlic, wine, clothes, birds, artichokes, socks, corn, and tuna. Think about something that you use, own, or eat that is an unsung hero, and elevate and honor it in a poem, no matter how small or seemingly insignificant.

Prompt 236

I CAN'T DO IT

Write a poem that consists of at least 10 couplets. Begin the first line of every couplet with the words "I can't...." and begin the second line of each couplet with the word "because." Before you begin this poem, relax and slow down your mind. As your write, allow the words to flow without much logical thought or editing. If you begin to feel anger or sadness as you continuously write "I can't…" let yourself create from the emotion. When you have completed the couplets, remove "I can't" and "because" from each line and see how your poem reads. Continue to revise until your poem feels complete.

Prompt 237

POET LIVES A LIFE ON CHOCOLATE AND COFFEE

Write a poem based on a tabloid-style news headline. It could be something such as "Fat Rat Trapped in Manhole Cover" or "Bat Boy Leads Cops on 3 State Chase" or "Abraham Lincoln was a Woman" or "House Cat Turns Owners into Slaves," etc. Scan some online tabloid news sites for ideas or do an online search for strange news stories. If you can't find a headline to inspire, feel free to make up your own.

Prompt 238

L IS FOR LOVE

Write a poem about something you love where every line begins with the same letter. Include as many active verbs as you can and similar vowel sounds. The lines can be as long or short as you need them to be, and each line does not need to be a separate sentence—it's okay for sentences to begin in one line and end in another. For extra credit, end the line with the same letter or sound.

Prompt 239

LET ME TELL YOU ABOUT...

Write a poem about something you've never written about. It can be a personal experience or a subject such as blacksmiths, buffalo, horror movies, tin cans. As you write about your chosen topic, continue to bring in words you have never used in a poem. If you are looking for some ideas, try including one or more of these words: *doohickey, galloping, asparagus, gridlock, alien, doodle, ass, nebula, gravy, gecko, Oz, widget, alchemy, zippy, goblin, skylight, plunger, vulture, milkweed, sauerkraut.*

Prompt 240

I BELIEVE THE CLOTHESPINS
ARE THE FUTURE

Write a poem that begins, "Tonight, I believe in…" but have the object(s) you believe in be something unexpected, like barbells, whiskey, skylines, bathing suits, or mini shampoos. Go deep into the details of one item, or write a list poem where each line contains something you believe in. Remember to list items that will surprise your reader.

About the Authors

Kelli Russell Agodon is the cofounder of Two Sylvias Press where she works as an editor and book cover designer. Her most recent book, *Hourglass Museum*, was a finalist for the Washington State Book Awards and shortlisted for the Julie Suk Poetry Prize. Her second book, *Letters from the Emily Dickinson Room* won Foreword Indies Book of the Year Prize for poetry. She coauthored *The Daily Poet: Day-By-Day Prompts for Your Writing Practice* with poet Martha Silano and is the Co-Director of Poets on the Coast. Her next collection of poems, *Dialogues with Rising Tides,* is forthcoming from Copper Canyon Press in 2021.

Annette Spaulding-Convy is a poet and editor in the Seattle area. Her full-length collection, *In Broken Latin*, was published by the University of Arkansas Press as a finalist for the Miller Williams Poetry Prize. Her chapbook *In the Convent We Become Clouds* won the Floating Bridge Press Chapbook Award. She was chosen for the Jack Straw Writer's Program and is a recipient of the Artist Trust GAP Grant and the Artist Trust Fellowship. She is cofounder and coeditor of Two Sylvias Press.

Founded in 2010 by Kelli Russell Agodon and Annette Spaulding-Convy, Two Sylvias is an independent press located in the Seattle area. We publish poetry, memoir, essays, books on the craft of writing, and creativity tools, such as *The Poet Tarot*, *The Daily Poet*, and *Everything is Writable*. Please visit Two Sylvias Press (www.twosylviaspress.com) for information on purchasing our print books, eBooks, writing tools, and for submission guidelines for our annual book prizes (Chapbook Prize and Wilder Prize).

Publications by Two Sylvias Press:

The Daily Poet: Day-By-Day Prompts For Your Writing Practice
by Kelli Russell Agodon and Martha Silano (Print and eBook)

The Daily Poet Companion Journal (Print)

Fire On Her Tongue: An Anthology of Contemporary Women's Poetry
edited by Kelli Russell Agodon and Annette Spaulding-Convy (Print and eBook)

The Poet Tarot and Guidebook: A Deck Of Creative Exploration (Print)

Everything is Writable: 240 Poetry Prompts from Two Sylvias Press
by Kelli Russell Agodon & Annette Spaulding-Convy (Print)

Crown of Wild, Winner of the 2018 Two Sylvias Press Wilder Prize
by Erica Bodwell (Print)

American Zero, Winner of the 2018 Two Sylvias Press Chapbook Prize
by Stella Wong (Print and eBook)

The Inspired Poet: Writing Exercises to Spark New Work
by Susan Landgraf (Print)

All Transparent Things Need Thundershirts, Winner of the 2017 Two Sylvias Press Wilder Prize
by Dana Roeser (Print and eBook)

Where The Horse Takes Wing: The Uncollected Poems of Madeline DeFrees
edited by Anne McDuffie (Print and eBook)

In The House Of My Father, Winner of the 2017 Two Sylvias Press Chapbook Prize by Hiwot Adilow (Print and eBook)

Box, Winner of the 2017 Two Sylvias Press Poetry Prize
by Sue D. Burton (Print and eBook)

Tsigan: The Gypsy Poem (New Edition)
by Cecilia Woloch (Print and eBook)

PR For Poets
by Jeannine Hall Gailey (Print and eBook)

Appalachians Run Amok, Winner of the 2016 Two Sylvias Press
Wilder Prize
by Adrian Blevins (Print and eBook)

Pass It On!
by Gloria J. McEwen Burgess (Print)

Killing Marias
by Claudia Castro Luna (Print and eBook)

The Ego and the Empiricist, Finalist 2016 Two Sylvias Press
Chapbook Prize
by Derek Mong (Print and eBook)

The Authenticity Experiment
by Kate Carroll de Gutes (Print and eBook)

Mytheria, Finalist 2015 Two Sylvias Press Wilder Prize
by Molly Tenenbaum (Print and eBook)

Arab in Newsland , Winner of the 2016 Two Sylvias Press
Chapbook Prize
by Lena Khalaf Tuffaha (Print and eBook)

The Blue Black Wet of Wood, Winner of the 2015 Two Sylvias
Press Wilder Prize
by Carmen R. Gillespie (Print and eBook)

Fire Girl: Essays on India, America, and the In-Between
by Sayantani Dasgupta (Print and eBook)

Blood Song
by Michael Schmeltzer (Print and eBook)

Naming The No-Name Woman,
Winner of the 2015 Two Sylvias Press Chapbook Prize
by Jasmine An (Print and eBook)

Community Chest
by Natalie Serber (Print)

Phantom Son: A Mother's Story of Surrender
by Sharon Estill Taylor (Print and eBook)

What The Truth Tastes Like
by Martha Silano (Print and eBook)

landscape/heartbreak
by Michelle Peñaloza (Print and eBook)

Earth, Winner of the 2014 Two Sylvias Press Chapbook Prize
by Cecilia Woloch (Print and eBook)

The Cardiologist's Daughter
by Natasha Kochicheril Moni (Print and eBook)

She Returns to the Floating World
by Jeannine Hall Gailey (Print and eBook)

Hourglass Museum
by Kelli Russell Agodon (eBook)

Cloud Pharmacy
by Susan Rich (eBook)

Dear Alzheimer's: A Caregiver's Diary & Poems
by Esther Altshul Helfgott (eBook)

Listening to Mozart: Poems of Alzheimer's
by Esther Altshul Helfgott (eBook)

Crab Creek Review 30th Anniversary Issue
featuring Northwest Poets
edited by Kelli Russell Agodon and Annette Spaulding-Convy
(eBook)

Made in the USA
Middletown, DE
13 July 2020